First Workshop on Performance and Interpretability Evaluations of Multimodal, Multipurpose, Massive-Scale Models (MMMPIE 2022)

Gyeongju, South Korea
12 – 17 October 2022

ISBN: 978-1-7138-6192-8

Printed from e-media with permission by:

Curran Associates, Inc.
57 Morehouse Lane
Red Hook, NY 12571

Some format issues inherent in the e-media version may also appear in this print version.

Printed with permission by Curran Associates, Inc. (2023)

Association for Computational Linguistics
209 N. Eighth Street
Stroudsburg, Pennsylvania 18360

Phone: 1-570-476-8006
Fax: 1-570-476-0860

acl@aclweb.org

Additional copies of this publication are available from:

Curran Associates, Inc.
57 Morehouse Lane
Red Hook, NY 12571 USA
Phone: 845-758-0400
Fax: 845-758-2633
Email: curran@proceedings.com
Web: www.proceedings.com

ACL 2020

The 29th International Conference on Computational Linguistics

Proceedings of the First Workshop on Performance and Interpretability Evaluations of Multimodal, Multipurpose, Massive-Scale Models (MMMPIE 2022)

October 12–17, 2022

Order copies of this and other ACL proceedings from:

Association for Computational Linguistics (ACL)
209 N. Eighth Street
Stroudsburg, PA 18360
USA
Tel: +1-570-476-8006
Fax: +1-570-476-0860
acl@aclweb.org

Organizing Committee

- Maria Glenski, Pacific Northwest National Laboratory
- Vidhisha Balachandran, Carnegie Mellon University
- Megan Kohagen, Quantinuum
- Yulia Tsvetkov, University of Washington

Table of Contents

Conference Program

On the Effects of Video Grounding on Language Models
Ehsan Doostmohammadi and Marco Kuhlmann

Rethinking Task Sampling for Few-shot Vision-Language Transfer Learning
Zhenhailong Wang, Hang Yu, Manling Li, Han Zhao and Heng Ji

Analyzing BERT Cross-lingual Transfer Capabilities in Continual Sequence Labeling
Juan Manuel Coria, Mathilde Veron, Sahar Ghannay, Guillaume Bernard, Hervé Bredin, Olivier Galibert and Sophie Rosset

Pixel-Level BPE for Auto-Regressive Image Generation
Anton Razzhigaev, Anton Voronov, Andrey Kaznacheev, Andrey Kuznetsov, Denis Dimitrov and Alexander Panchenko

Cost-Effective Language Driven Image Editing with LX-DRIM
Rodrigo Santos, António Branco and João Ricardo Silva

Shapes of Emotions: Multimodal Emotion Recognition in Conversations via Emotion Shifts
Keshav Bansal, Harsh Agarwal, Abhinav Joshi and Ashutosh Modi

On the Effects of Video Grounding on Language Models

Ehsan Doostmohammadi and **Marco Kuhlmann**
Linköping University, Linköping, Sweden
{ehsan.doostmohammadi, marco.kuhlmann}@liu.se

Abstract

Transformer-based models trained on text and vision modalities try to improve the performance on multimodal downstream tasks or tackle the problem of lack of grounding, e.g., addressing issues like models' insufficient commonsense knowledge. While it is more straightforward to evaluate the effects of such models on multimodal tasks, such as visual question answering or image captioning, it is not as well-understood how these tasks affect the model itself, and its internal linguistic representations. In this work, we experiment with language models grounded in videos and measure the models' performance on predicting masked words chosen based on their *imageability*. The results show that the smaller model benefits from video grounding in predicting highly imageable words, while the results for the larger model seem harder to interpret.

1 Introduction

A traditional language model is only exposed to textual data. While ample information exists in the form of text, some text-external knowledge might be missing, such as commonsense knowledge about the physical world, how objects look like, relate to each other, and how we interact with them. There is an abundance of work on trying to expose language models to other information sources and modalities, or in other words, grounding them; however, it is not clear how that would affect a language model in general. One promising modality to ground language models in is vision. Previous work has studied the grounding of language models in visual input and how this affects their performance on downstream multimodal tasks, such as visual question answering and image retrieval (Touvron et al., 2021; Li et al., 2020b; Lu et al., 2019; Su et al., 2019), and on models' "understanding" of the world and their grasp of commonsense knowledge (Sileo, 2021; Hendricks and Nematzadeh, 2021; Norlund et al., 2021).

Our aim with this work is to see whether *grounding in videos* affects the performance of transformer-based language models on masked lnaguage modeling. Masked language modeling is the task of predicting one or more masked tokens, given other tokens in the sentence. Evaluating a model's performance on such cloze-test-style fill-in-the-blank tasks is simple to implement and does not require expensive annotated data. Still, it can provide us with helpful intuition about how models work. This method also makes it easy to compare language models grounded in different modalities without further fine-tuning them. We choose to experiment with videos rather than images because they contain more information about the physical world, and may be more useful for the development of spatial, temporal and causal reasoning. Videos are also less studied in the literature.

The masked words that we want the model to predict are chosen based on their *imageability*. Imageability is a well-established notion from the field of psychology, defined as "the ease with which a word gives rise to a sensory mental image" (Paivio et al., 1968). For instance, words like "to prance" and "oven" are considered highly imageable, while words like "to consider" and "problem" are not. Imageability is highly correlated with concreteness, but the class of imageable words also includes abstract words, e.g. emotion words such as "anger". At the same time, this class does not include less experienced, yet concrete, words such as "armadillo" (Paivio et al., 1968). We use a dataset consisting of 2,645 words annotated with their imageability scores (Bird et al., 2001) to experiment with different types of models and investigate whether there is a performance difference between grounded and not grounded language models when predicting low-imageability versus high-imageability words. The words in our dataset are labeled with their parts-of-speech, which we will use in our experiments and analysis of the results.

Proceedings of the 29th International Conference on Computational Linguistics, pages 1–6
October 12–17, 2022.

We continue the paper with explaining the models' architecture in §2 and the data sets used in §3. The experimental settings and the results are described in §4, where we also analyze the results and try to interpret them. In §5 we briefly discuss some related work.

2 Model

We mainly follow the data preprocessing steps, the architecture, and the training regime of VideoBERT model (Sun et al., 2019). We experiment with a pre-trained BERT-base model (Vaswani et al., 2017) and DistilBERT (Sanh et al., 2019). BERT is essentially a transformer-based model (Vaswani et al., 2017) pretrained with masked language modeling and next sentence prediction objectives, and DistilBERT is the distilled version of the BERT model, which has half the number of layers as BERT-base. Both language models are pretrained on the same data.

As for the video features, we use the I3D model pre-trained on the Kinetics dataset (Carreira and Zisserman, 2017) to encode video clips that are sampled at 20 fps and are 1.5 seconds long. We then apply hierarchical k-means clustering to the video features, setting the number of hierarchy levels to 4 and the number of clusters per level k to 12, which results in $12^4 = 20{,}736$ clusters. Henceforth, we use the closest cluster centroids as video tokens instead of continuous video features. As the output of the I3D model is of size 600, we use a fully connected layer to map to the embedding size of the respective model.

We further train the pre-trained language models with a masked language modeling training objective with a masking probability of 0.15 for each modality. The embeddings of the word tokens (w_i) and the video tokens (v_j) are concatenated with a new special token [>] as the text–video separator. This results in an input I of the form

$$I = ([\text{CLS}], w_1, ..., w_n, [>], v_1, ..., v_m, [\text{SEP}])$$

The [CLS] and [SEP] tokens are the models' special tokens for classification and separation of sentences, respectively. The embedding weights and video features are frozen during training. The input I is then fed to the model to get the output O, which is mapped to the vocabulary space by means of a projection layer consisting of two fully connected layers (FC) and layer normalization:

$$\hat{y} = FC_2(LN(FC_1(O)))$$

All the new layers and embedding weights are initialized randomly from a uniform distribution (He et al., 2015). The final objective is to maximize the log-likelihood $\sum_{l=1}^{L} \log p(\hat{y}_l \mid x_{\setminus l}; \theta)$, where l is the masked token, and the xs are the input tokens, text or video, without the lth token. Special tokens are never masked.

We train two models with almost the same architecture, as described above, once only with textual input, and once with text and video input. The only difference in the structures is that the text model lacks the projection layer, which makes comparison between the models possible. The random seed is the same for both models all the time and changes by epoch. The models are trained using the Adam optimizer with a learning rate of 10^{-5} and batch size of 2^{10}. We stop the training when the model's loss and accuracy plateaus on the validation set.

The implementations and the pretrained weights of the Hugging Face Transformer library (Wolf et al., 2019) are used in these experiments.

3 Data

To get imageability scores for nouns and verbs, we use Bird's dataset, in which words with different parts-of-speech, are rated with imageability scores from 100 to 700. For training and testing the models, HowTo100M (Miech et al., 2019) dataset is used, which is a collection of 1.2M narrated English YouTube videos from various categories. We randomly choose 55K videos from the dataset and split these into 45K videos for training, 5K for development, and 5K for testing, or in other words 4.7M samples for training and ~500K for the other sets. To get some idea on how the HowTo100M data looks, we measure the mean imageability score on a random set of 300K tokens from the dataset, which was 454 on type level, and 366 on token level, which shows a high frequency of low imageability words in the dataset.

There are a total of 892 verb types and 1,304 noun types in the Bird dataset. We split the words in the Bird dataset into low imageability (≤ 300) and high imageability (≥ 500) ones. This results in 114 low imageability and 511 high imageability types, or 67K and 92K tokens, respectively. The type-token ratio for low imageability words is 17×10^{-4}, while being 55×10^{-4} for highly imageable ones.

	Train	Test	Imageability	Accuracy (Δ)	N. Acc. (Δ)	V. Acc. (Δ)
DistilBERT	Baseline		Low	22.1	22.8	22.1
			High	10.1	10.5	9.4
	T	T	Low	34.3	24.0	35.7
			High	16.8	16.6	17.5
	TV	TV	Low	33.7 (-0.6)	23.7 (-0.3)	35.0 (-0.7)
			High	17.7 (0.9)	17.2 (0.6)	18.9 (1.4)
	TV	T	Low	34.1 (-0.2)	24.0 (0.0)	35.5 (0.2)
			High	17.1 (0.3)	16.7 (0.1)	18.0 (0.5)
BERT	Baseline		Low	24.4	23.7	24.4
			High	10.8	12.4	7.5
	T	T	Low	38.6	32.8	38.6
			High	21.4	21.5	21.2
	TV	TV	Low	39.1 (0.5)	32.9 (0.1)	39.6 (1.0)
			High	21.9 (0.5)	21.8 (0.3)	22.0 (0.8)
	TV	T	Low	39.3 (0.7)	33.0 (0.2)	39.7 (1.2)
			High	21.0 (-0.4)	21.1 (-0.4)	20.7 (-0.5)

Table 1: Accuracy on low and high imageability words for the DistilBERT and BERT models. The results columns are for the overall accuracy (noun and verb), the noun accuracy, and the verb accuracy, respectively. The Δ is the difference between that result and the corresponding result (in terms of imageability) of the T-T model. The baseline is the model with pre-trained weights, but not fine-tuned on this dataset. For more details about the T and TV abbreviations refer to the text.

4 Results and Analysis

The model is fed with those sentences from the HowTo100M dataset that contains at least one word from Bird's dataset. For each sample, we only mask one noun or verb at a time to make the analysis simple. The experiments are done on two models and in three different settings:

(1) only textual input to the text-only model (T-T),

(2) text and video input to text and video model (TV-TV), and

(3) only text input to text and video model (TV-T).

The same settings are repeated for both DistilBERT and BERT-base models.

Table 1 contains the main token-level results of masked word prediction accuracy of the aforementioned three different scenarios on low and high imageability nouns and verbs. The overall accuracy is simply a weighted sum of the noun and verb accuracy. For DistilBERT, which is the smaller of the two models, the results show an increase in performance on high imageability when the model is grounded in videos (TV-TV). For the same scenario, but with low imageability words, we see some decrease in performance, which might be due to the model treating the video signal as noise. The performance goes up when removing the video from the input of the same model (TV-T). For high imageability words in the same TV-T setting, the results show some increase compared to the T-T setting, which might be due to the model learning information from the video input which is useful to masked word prediction task, even in the absence of the video signal.

On the other hand, for BERT, numbers are harder to interpret. We still see some increase for high imageability words, and more for verbs compared to nouns, but we see more or less the same amount of increase for low imageability words. It is hard to say why this is happening only for the BERT model, but one reason might be that the model receives more learning signals during training when the sequences are longer (TV), hence the higher number of masked tokens. Removing the video input from the input (TV-T) hurts the high imageability words the most, which shows the dependence of the model on the video signal. These results are not consistent with the DistilBERT model.

One should bear in mind that the relative increase in accuracy for high imageability words, e.g., between T-T and TV-TV, is higher than for low imageability ones, as the accuracy for low imageability words is always considerably higher than that of the high imageability ones. For example, an increase of 1.4% in high imageability verb prediction accuracy in the DistilBERT TV-TV model is a 7.4% relative increase, while 1.0% for BERT TV-TV low imageability verbs is only a 2.5%. One should also consider the fact that low imageability words have a much higher frequency in the data, which means the model has seen them more often. While the average imageability score in the Bird dataset is around 460, the average token-based imageability score is around 360 for Howto100M and some other datasets, including Violin (Liu et al., 2020), and TVQA subtitles (Lei et al., 2018).

The differences between different models' performances are not large, however, considering the size of the test set, they are quite significant. Additionally, a bootstrap test always shows a p-value of smaller than $3.9e-5$, which indicates a very high significance for all the results. We ran the bootstrap test as described in Berg-Kirkpatrick et al. (2012): a sample $x^{(i)}$ of the same size as the test set is drawn with replacement for $b = 10^6$ times, and p-value is calculated as s/b, where s is the number of times where $\delta(x^{(i)}) > 2\delta(x)$ holds. δ is the performance difference of systems A and B, and x is the original test set.

Comparing DistilBERT T-T and TV-TV shows that the words that benefit from the video signal are predominantly highly imageable ones, e.g., *add, cook, plant, hair, bottom, turn, pour, house, remove,* and *ground*, while low imageability words, such as *see, want, go, way, take,* and *like*, see a reduction in prediction accuracy. *Go* is a special verb in the sense that it typically appears as an auxiliary verb to indicate the future tense, which is low in imageability. When removing the video signal in BERT (TV-T), high imageability words see a reduction in accuracy, while it is the opposite for the low imageability ones. Interestingly, the top 30 words that benefit the most from the video signal in DistilBERT (TV-TV) have a 63% overlap with the ones that see the most reduction when removing the signal in BERT (TV-T). BERT (T-T) is already good at predicting the words (high or low in imageability), and does not benefit from the video signal as DistilBERT. However, training it on video signals apparently makes it more dependent on them for predicting high imageability words, so that removing the signal hurts the performance.

5 Related Work

Recent work on visual grounding has explored the effects of joint modeling of paired textual and visual modalities, with a focus on neural models based on the Transformer architecture (Frank et al., 2021; Li et al., 2020b; Chen et al., 2020; Huang et al., 2020; Lu et al., 2019). There is also some work that goes deeper into the problem, such as Sileo (2021), who studies the effects of visual grounding on text processing abilities of a language model using transferred and associative grounding, and how they improve text-only baselines, such as commonsense-related downstream tasks.

Another work is Hendricks and Nematzadeh (2021), who study how text-image pre-trained transformer models perform in situations that require "noun or verb understanding". According to them, such models perform poorly when evaluated on verbs compared to other parts of speech. Ebert and Pavlick (2020) experiment with an interactive simulated kitchen environment and conclude that certain machine learning models predict verbs less accurately than nouns, given a scene. They are motivated by work in psychology showing that predicting actions (verbs) is much harder than predicting objects (nouns) for people, given a video scene and the linguistic context of the word (Gillette et al., 1999).

In this work, we mainly followed VideoBERT (Sun et al., 2019), but there are other methods of integrating text and video as well. One other work is HERO (Li et al., 2020a), which does not use discretized video features, but continuous features with a regression loss. One other interesting work is ClipBERT (Lei et al., 2021), which tries to utilize sparse sampling to use fewer video frames to improve the text-video downstream tasks. There are also some work on joint representation of text and video, such as ActBERT (Zhu and Yang, 2020) and MIL-NCE (Miech et al., 2020).

6 Conclusion and Future Work

Although it is hard to draw strong conclusions based on these results, it might be that smaller models benefit more from video grounding than larger ones in the task of masked token prediction. The results are in line with the recent work on image grounding (Iki and Aizawa, 2021; Li et al., 2021), which suggests that the visual input might not be exploited by the model to the fullest. While the results are not strongly indicative, these models are relatively small and training data size is also minimal. The data size is chosen based on the results in Sun et al. (2019), who show that this much data should be enough to see some improvement. Increasing the data and model size could be a direction for future work. Another interesting research question that was not addressed in this paper is whether we really need to ground in videos for the model to gain the relevant knowledge, or can get the same results by using images or sampled key frame(s).

Acknowledgements

This work was partially supported by the Wallenberg AI, Autonomous Systems and Software Program (WASP) funded by the Knut and Alice Wallenberg Foundation. The computations and data handling were enabled by resources provided by the Swedish National Infrastructure for Computing (SNIC), partially funded by the Swedish Research Council through grant agreements no. 2021/7-111 and 2021/23-556, and by the Berzelius resources provided by the Knut and Alice Wallenberg Foundation at the National Supercomputer Centre.

References

Taylor Berg-Kirkpatrick, David Burkett, and Dan Klein. 2012. An empirical investigation of statistical significance in nlp. In *Proceedings of the 2012 Joint Conference on Empirical Methods in Natural Language Processing and Computational Natural Language Learning*, pages 995–1005.

Helen Bird, Sue Franklin, and David Howard. 2001. Age of acquisition and imageability ratings for a large set of words, including verbs and function words. *Behavior Research Methods, Instruments, & Computers*, 33(1):73–79.

Joao Carreira and Andrew Zisserman. 2017. Quo vadis, action recognition? a new model and the kinetics dataset. In *proceedings of the IEEE Conference on Computer Vision and Pattern Recognition*, pages 6299–6308.

Yen-Chun Chen, Linjie Li, Licheng Yu, Ahmed El Kholy, Faisal Ahmed, Zhe Gan, Yu Cheng, and Jingjing Liu. 2020. Uniter: Universal image-text representation learning. In *European conference on computer vision*, pages 104–120. Springer.

Dylan Ebert and Ellie Pavlick. 2020. A visuospatial dataset for naturalistic verb learning. In *Proceedings of the Ninth Joint Conference on Lexical and Computational Semantics*, pages 143–153, Barcelona, Spain (Online). Association for Computational Linguistics.

Stella Frank, Emanuele Bugliarello, and Desmond Elliott. 2021. Vision-and-language or vision-for-language? on cross-modal influence in multimodal transformers. In *Proceedings of the 2021 Conference on Empirical Methods in Natural Language Processing*, pages 9847–9857.

Jane Gillette, Henry Gleitman, Lila Gleitman, and Anne Lederer. 1999. Human simulations of vocabulary learning. *Cognition*, 73(2):135–176.

Kaiming He, Xiangyu Zhang, Shaoqing Ren, and Jian Sun. 2015. Delving deep into rectifiers: Surpassing human-level performance on imagenet classification. In *Proceedings of the IEEE international conference on computer vision*, pages 1026–1034.

Lisa Anne Hendricks and Aida Nematzadeh. 2021. Probing image-language transformers for verb understanding. In *Findings of the Association for Computational Linguistics: ACL-IJCNLP 2021*, pages 3635–3644.

Zhicheng Huang, Zhaoyang Zeng, Bei Liu, Dongmei Fu, and Jianlong Fu. 2020. Pixel-bert: Aligning image pixels with text by deep multi-modal transformers. *arXiv preprint arXiv:2004.00849*.

Taichi Iki and Akiko Aizawa. 2021. Effect of visual extensions on natural language understanding in vision-and-language models. In *Proceedings of the 2021 Conference on Empirical Methods in Natural Language Processing*, pages 2189–2196.

Jie Lei, Linjie Li, Luowei Zhou, Zhe Gan, Tamara L Berg, Mohit Bansal, and Jingjing Liu. 2021. Less is more: Clipbert for video-and-language learning via sparse sampling. In *Proceedings of the IEEE/CVF Conference on Computer Vision and Pattern Recognition*, pages 7331–7341.

Jie Lei, Licheng Yu, Mohit Bansal, and Tamara Berg. 2018. TVQA: Localized, compositional video question answering. In *Proceedings of the 2018 Conference on Empirical Methods in Natural Language Processing*, pages 1369–1379, Brussels, Belgium. Association for Computational Linguistics.

Jiaoda Li, Duygu Ataman, and Rico Sennrich. 2021. Vision matters when it should: Sanity checking multimodal machine translation models. In *Proceedings of the 2021 Conference on Empirical Methods in Natural Language Processing*, pages 8556–8562.

Linjie Li, Yen-Chun Chen, Yu Cheng, Zhe Gan, Licheng Yu, and Jingjing Liu. 2020a. HERO: Hierarchical encoder for Video+Language omni-representation pre-training. In *Proceedings of the 2020 Conference on Empirical Methods in Natural Language Processing (EMNLP)*, pages 2046–2065, Online. Association for Computational Linguistics.

Xiujun Li, Xi Yin, Chunyuan Li, Pengchuan Zhang, Xiaowei Hu, Lei Zhang, Lijuan Wang, Houdong Hu, Li Dong, Furu Wei, et al. 2020b. Oscar: Object-semantics aligned pre-training for vision-language tasks. In *European Conference on Computer Vision*, pages 121–137. Springer.

Jingzhou Liu, Wenhu Chen, Yu Cheng, Zhe Gan, Licheng Yu, Yiming Yang, and Jingjing Liu. 2020. Violin: A large-scale dataset for video-and-language inference. In *Proceedings of the IEEE/CVF Conference on Computer Vision and Pattern Recognition*, pages 10900–10910.

Jiasen Lu, Dhruv Batra, Devi Parikh, and Stefan Lee. 2019. Vilbert: Pretraining task-agnostic visiolinguistic representations for vision-and-language tasks. *Advances in neural information processing systems*, 32.

Antoine Miech, Jean-Baptiste Alayrac, Lucas Smaira, Ivan Laptev, Josef Sivic, and Andrew Zisserman. 2020. End-to-End Learning of Visual Representations from Uncurated Instructional Videos. In *CVPR*.

Antoine Miech, Dimitri Zhukov, Jean-Baptiste Alayrac, Makarand Tapaswi, Ivan Laptev, and Josef Sivic. 2019. HowTo100M: Learning a Text-Video Embedding by Watching Hundred Million Narrated Video Clips. In *ICCV*.

Tobias Norlund, Lovisa Hagström, and Richard Johansson. 2021. Transferring knowledge from vision to language: How to achieve it and how to measure it? In *Proceedings of the Fourth BlackboxNLP Workshop on Analyzing and Interpreting Neural Networks for NLP*, pages 149–162.

Allan Paivio, John C Yuille, and Stephen A Madigan. 1968. Concreteness, imagery, and meaningfulness values for 925 nouns. *Journal of experimental psychology*, 76(1p2):1.

Victor Sanh, Lysandre Debut, Julien Chaumond, and Thomas Wolf. 2019. Distilbert, a distilled version of bert: smaller, faster, cheaper and lighter. *arXiv preprint arXiv:1910.01108*.

Damien Sileo. 2021. Visual grounding strategies for text-only natural language processing. In *Proceedings of the Third Workshop on Beyond Vision and LANguage: inTEgrating Real-world kNowledge (LANTERN)*, pages 19–29.

Weijie Su, Xizhou Zhu, Yue Cao, Bin Li, Lewei Lu, Furu Wei, and Jifeng Dai. 2019. Vl-bert: Pre-training of generic visual-linguistic representations. *arXiv preprint arXiv:1908.08530*.

Chen Sun, Austin Myers, Carl Vondrick, Kevin Murphy, and Cordelia Schmid. 2019. Videobert: A joint model for video and language representation learning. In *Proceedings of the IEEE/CVF International Conference on Computer Vision*, pages 7464–7473.

Hugo Touvron, Matthieu Cord, Matthijs Douze, Francisco Massa, Alexandre Sablayrolles, and Hervé Jégou. 2021. Training data-efficient image transformers & distillation through attention. In *International Conference on Machine Learning*, pages 10347–10357. PMLR.

Ashish Vaswani, Noam Shazeer, Niki Parmar, Jakob Uszkoreit, Llion Jones, Aidan N Gomez, Łukasz Kaiser, and Illia Polosukhin. 2017. Attention is all you need. *Advances in neural information processing systems*, 30.

Thomas Wolf, Lysandre Debut, Victor Sanh, Julien Chaumond, Clement Delangue, Anthony Moi, Pierric Cistac, Tim Rault, Rémi Louf, Morgan Funtowicz, et al. 2019. Huggingface's transformers: State-of-the-art natural language processing. *arXiv preprint arXiv:1910.03771*.

Linchao Zhu and Yi Yang. 2020. Actbert: Learning global-local video-text representations. In *Proceedings of the IEEE/CVF conference on computer vision and pattern recognition*, pages 8746–8755.

Rethinking Task Sampling for Few-shot Vision-Language Transfer Learning

Zhenhailong Wang, Hang Yu, Manling Li, Han Zhao, Heng Ji
University of Illinois at Urbana-Champaign
{wangz3, hengji}@illinois.edu

Abstract

Despite achieving state-of-the-art zero-shot performance, existing vision-language models still fall short of few-shot transfer ability on domain-specific problems. Classical fine-tuning often fails to prevent highly expressive models from exploiting spurious correlations in the training data. Although model-agnostic meta-learning (MAML) presents as a natural alternative for few-shot transfer learning, the expensive computation due to implicit second-order optimization limits its use on large-scale vision-language models such as CLIP. While much literature has been devoted to exploring alternative optimization strategies, we identify another essential aspect towards effective few-shot transfer learning, *task sampling*, which is previously only be viewed as part of data pre-processing in MAML. To show the impact of task sampling, we propose a simple algorithm, Model-Agnostic Multitask Fine-tuning (MAMF), which differentiates classical fine-tuning only on uniformly sampling multiple tasks. Despite its simplicity, we show that MAMF consistently outperforms classical fine-tuning on five few-shot image classification tasks. We further show that the effectiveness of the bi-level optimization in MAML is highly sensitive to the zero-shot performance of a task in the context of few-shot vision-language classification. The goal of this paper is to provide new insights on what makes few-shot learning work, and encourage more research into investigating better task sampling strategies.

1 Introduction

While existing machine learning models have achieved human-level performance at various individual tasks, they generally lack the ability of fast adaptation and generalization. In recent years, transfer learning has been proven to be effective on a wide range of Computer Vision (He et al., 2016; Dosovitskiy et al., 2020) and Natural Language Processing (Devlin et al., 2019; Lewis et al., 2020) tasks. Specifically, recent advances in large-scale vision-language models (Radford et al., 2021; Jia et al., 2021; Li et al., 2022; Alayrac et al., 2022) have demonstrated strong zero-shot ability on a wide range of tasks. However, these models still have certain limitations on concepts that require extensive domain knowledge, such as Fungi Classification. We identify two major limitations in current few-shot transfer learning literature, from both evaluation and algorithm perspectives.

Limitation on evaluation: In current transfer learning paradigm, the testing instances of a downstream task are drawn from the same distribution as the training set. This evaluation setting can fail to faithfully reflect whether a model has truly learned a new concept, since modern deep neural networks can easily memorize and exploit spurious correlations from the training set (Brown et al., 2020). Thus, we first propose a new evaluation scheme for *few-shot transfer learning* where we replace the original testing phase with *meta-testing* (Section 3). With *meta-testing*, the testing distribution are distinguished from the training.

Limitation on algorithm: To make an arbitrary pretrained vision-language model learn new concepts with few examples, model-agnostic meta-learning (MAML) (Finn et al., 2017) presents as a natural candidate. One major limitation of the original MAML method is the expensive computation overhead due to implicit second-order optimization. Most follow-up work (Finn et al., 2017; Nichol et al., 2018; Rajeswaran et al., 2019; Raghu et al., 2020; Von Oswald et al., 2021) has focused on improving the optimization strategy. However, we found that they all achieved comparable performance despite of using different optimization algorithms. This observation motivates us to ask: *If the specific choice of optimization method is not the key to the empirical success of MAML, what would be?*

Inspired by related work in the area of multitask

Proceedings of the 29th International Conference on Computational Linguistics, pages 7–14
October 12–17, 2022.

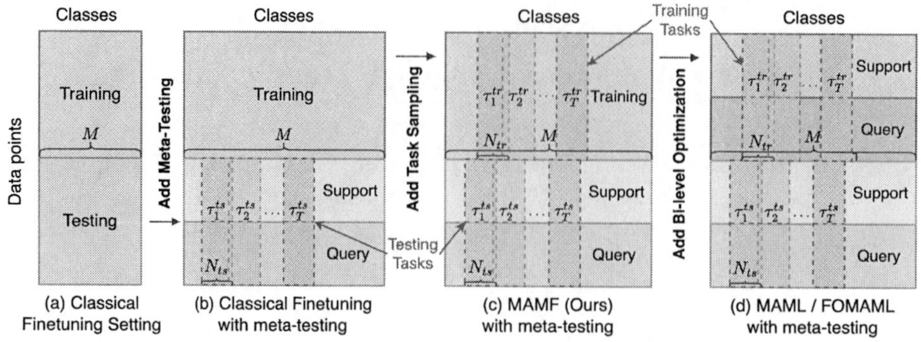

Figure 1: Task sampling and optimization schemes of different algorithms. Evaluation with meta-testing is applied in all of our experiments (b,c,d). Please find the detailed formulation in Section 3.

learning (Maurer et al., 2016; Tripuraneni et al., 2020), we conjecture that *task sampling* itself is an essential ingredient in learning new concepts efficiently. To verify this hypothesis, we propose a simple fine-tuning algorithm, *Model-Agnostic Multitask Fine-tuning (MAMF)*, which simplifies MAML by using only first-order gradient-based optimization while keeping the uniform task sampling procedure intact. The goal is **NOT** to propose yet another complex algorithm, but to investigate what is the most important aspect for effective few-shot transfer learning. We compare MAMF with Classical Fine-tuning, which does not perform uniform task sampling, and first-order MAML (FO-MAML) (Finn et al., 2017), which adopts complex bi-level optimization upon sampled tasks. Our empirical result demonstrates the importance of ***uniform task sampling*** and reveals limited effectiveness of the bi-level optimization of MAML in the context of few-shot transfer learning. We hope our work encourages more research into exploring better task sampling strategies for improving few-shot transfer learning and meta-learning algorithms.

2 Problem Formulation

We are interested in a few-shot classification problem where we have a pretrained vision-language model f with initial parameters $\boldsymbol{\theta}$. Let τ^{tr} be a training task sampled from a distribution $p(\tau^{tr})$, and τ^{ts} be a testing task sampled from $p(\tau^{ts})$, where a **task** is defined to an **induced sub-problem by restricting the output space from the original problem**. Specifically, for an original classification problem with M classes in total, we define a task as a sub-problem where the output space is a subset of N classes randomly sampled from the M classes. We further denote N^{tr} and N^{ts} as the number of classes in each training and testing task. T^{tr} and T^{ts} as the total number of sampled tasks respectively. The Classical Fine-tuning setting is depicted in Figure 1 (a), where we have $T^{tr} = 1$ training tasks with $N^{tr} = M$ classes, and $T^{ts} = 1$ testing tasks with $N^{ts} = M$ classes. That is, both training and testing sets are treated as one single task containing data points from all M classes.

3 Reformulating Classical Fine-tuning Evaluation with Meta-testing

Our goal is to enable and evaluate a model's capability of generalizing to new concepts with few examples. The Classical Fine-tuning setting is not sufficient since the training and testing data points are drawn from the same distribution. Therefore, we propose to replace the original joint testing in Classical Fine-tuning with *meta-testing*.

Meta-testing is first introduced by related work in meta-learning (Thrun and Pratt, 2012; Vinyals et al., 2016; Finn et al., 2017). As shown in the testing phase of Figure 1 (b,c,d), we first sample T^{ts} tasks ($T^{ts} > 1$), each containing data points from N^{ts} classes ($1 < N^{ts} < M$). For each sampled testing task τ^{ts}, we further randomly split the data points into two disjoint sets, i.e., support set A and query set B, with corresponding loss $\mathcal{L}_{\tau^{ts},A}$ and $\mathcal{L}_{\tau^{ts},B}$. Then we further update the model parameters on the support set and evaluate on the query set. By randomly sampling multiple tasks during *meta-testing*, we can distinguish the testing distribution from training, which largely prevents the model from exploiting spurious correlations in the training set. Essentially, we make the original problem more challenging by requiring the model to quickly generalize to potentially unseen task distributions during testing. The objective is to find an updated model parameter $\widetilde{\theta}$ that minimizes the expected loss on all testing tasks $\mathbb{E}_{\mathcal{T}^{ts} \sim p(\mathcal{T}^{ts})}\left[\mathcal{L}_{\mathcal{T}^{ts}}(\widetilde{\theta})\right]$. Specifically, under this setting, MAML's objective can be written as follows:

$$\min_{\widetilde{\theta}} \mathbb{E}_{\mathcal{T}^{ts} \sim p(\mathcal{T}^{ts})}\left[\mathcal{L}_{\mathcal{T}^{ts},B}\left(U^{ts}_{\mathcal{T}^{ts},A}(\widetilde{\theta})\right)\right],$$
$$\widetilde{\theta} = \min_{\theta} \mathbb{E}_{\mathcal{T}^{tr} \sim p(\mathcal{T}^{tr})}\left[\mathcal{L}_{\mathcal{T}^{tr},B}\left(U^{tr}_{\mathcal{T}^{tr},A}(\theta)\right)\right]$$

where $U^{tr}_{\mathcal{T}^{tr},A}$ is the optimization procedure that updates the initial parameter θ for one or more steps on the support set of a training task $\mathcal{T}^{tr}$.

4 Model-Agnostic Multitask Fine-tuning

As shown above, previous MAML-like methods update model parameters iteratively via a complex bi-level optimization scheme (Finn et al., 2017; Raghu et al., 2020; Rajeswaran et al., 2019), which is computationally expensive. We hypothesize that the *task sampling* process itself is more important than specific choice of optimization method. To verify this hypothesis, we propose a simple algorithm, *Model-Agnostic Multitask Fine-tuning (MAMF)*, where we keep the uniform task sampling strategy as MAML but perform simple first-order gradient-based optimization on each task sequentially. Unlike MAML, MAMF does not further split the tasks into support and query sets. The objective of MAMF can be written as:

$$\min_{\widetilde{\theta}} \mathbb{E}_{\mathcal{T}^{ts} \sim p(\mathcal{T}^{ts})}\left[\mathcal{L}_{\mathcal{T}^{ts},B}\left(U^{ts}_{\mathcal{T}^{ts},A}(\widetilde{\theta})\right)\right]$$
$$\widetilde{\theta} = \theta_{i=T^{tr}}, \theta_i = U^{tr}_{\mathcal{T}^{tr}_i}(\theta_{i-1}), i \in \{1, 2, ..., T^{tr}\}$$

where $\theta_0 = \theta$ and $U^{tr}_{\mathcal{T}^{tr}_i}$ is the optimization procedure that updates the parameters from the previous task on the current training task $\mathcal{T}^{tr}_i$. MAMF can also be viewed as a simplified version of Reptile (Nichol et al., 2018), where we further eliminate the hyper-parameter of step size. The goal is to keep the algorithm as simple as possible to distinguish the impact of *task sampling*. Figure 1 depicts a comparison of different data sampling and optimization schemes of different algorithms.

5 Experiment

5.1 Experimental Setup

We aim to investigate two main questions experimentally under **a few-shot vision-language transfer learning setting**:

- **Q1**: Is the *uniform task sampling* during training important?
- **Q2**: Is the *bi-level optimization* in MAML consistently effective?

To answer the first question, we compare MAMF with Classical Fine-tuning where the only difference is the additional uniform task sampling. For the second question, we compare FOMAML[1] and MAMF.

We perform comprehensive experiments on five few-shot image-classification datasets with various domains, including ClevrCounting (Johnson et al., 2017), Amazon Berkeley Objects (ABO) (Collins et al., 2021) Material, Fungi (Su et al., 2021), Mini-Imagenet (Vinyals et al., 2016), Caltech-UCSD Birds 200 (CUB) (Welinder et al., 2010). We compare different learning algorithms by applying them to a large-scale vision-language model, i.e., CLIP (Radford et al., 2021). We adopt the contrastive classification framework following (Radford et al., 2021) where we directly match prompted label text with encoded images. This framework allows us to avoid the label permutation problem raised by (Ye and Chao, 2021). Details on the datasets and the classification framework can be found in Appendix A and B.

Given a dataset with M classes in total, we experiment with various task configurations regarding the number of sub-sampled classes N^{ts}, where $2 \leq N^{ts} \leq M$. That is, during *meta-testing*, each task can be formulated as a N^{ts}-way classification and we randomly sample T^{ts} such tasks. During training, for Classical Fine-tuning, we set the training task configuration as $N^{tr} = M, T^{tr} = 1$; for MAMF and FOMAML, we set $N^{tr} = N^{ts} = N, T^{tr} = T^{ts} = T$, where T is determined based on N to cover all classes with a high probability. Implementation details can be found in Appendix C.

5.2 Results

Answer to Q1: Uniform task sampling is important. As depicted in Figure 2, comparing the performance of MAMF (red line) and Classical Fine-tuning (yellow line), MAMF consistently outperforms Classical Fine-tuning on all five datasets. Recall that the only difference between MAMF and Classical Fine-tuning is whether they perform uniform task sampling during training. This empirical

[1]We use the first-order variant of MAML for apple-to-apple comparison with MAMF.

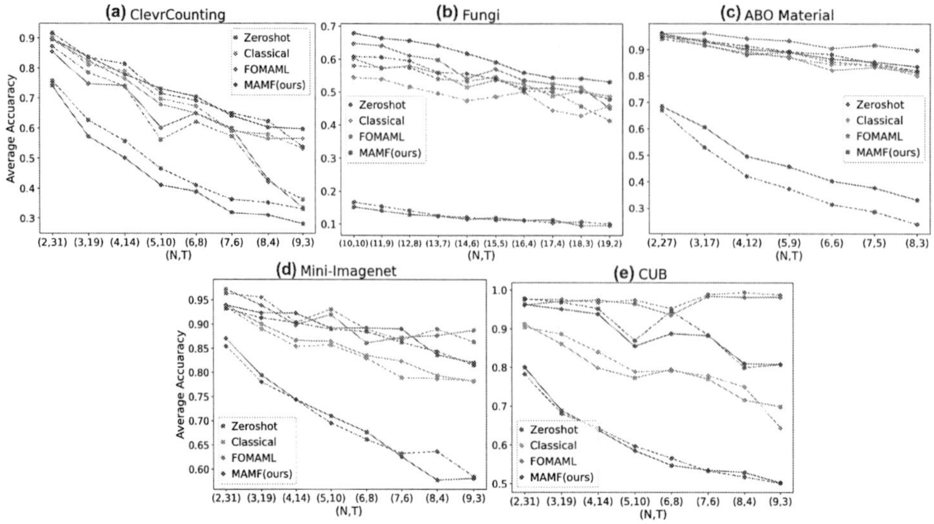

Figure 2: Average accuracy on development sets (*dashed* line) and test sets (*solid* line) of five datasets. The x-axis shows the task configurations where (N, T) refers to sampling T tasks for N-way classification. *Zeroshot* refers to zero-shot CLIP without any fine-tuning during either training or meta-testing. *Classical* refers to classical fine-tuning which treats the entire training set as a single task. Both *FOMAML* and *MAMF* sample N-way T tasks during training. *MAMF* consistently outperforms *Classical* on all datasets. Detailed scores can be found in Table 3.

result shows that task sampling itself serves as an important procedure for learning new concepts in a few-shot setting, even if with its simplest form, i.e. uniform sampling.

Answer to Q2: MAML is not effective on learning initially challenging problems. One unexpected observation from Figure 2 is that, although FOMAML has the same task sampling procedure and more sophisticated optimization method than MAMF, it is outperformed by MAMF on many tasks. We find that the effectiveness of FOMAML is highly sensitive to the zero-shot performance of the target task. Whenever the task is initially more challenging, i.e., with lower zero-shot performance, FOMAML tends to be less effective. For example, on CUB (Figure 2 e) where the zero-shot accuracy ranges from 0.5 to 0.8, FOMAML outperforms other algorithms in most cases. However, on ClevrCounting (Figure 2 a) where the zero-shot accuracy ranges from 0.3 to 0.75, MAMF and even Classical Fine-tuning consistently outperform FOMAML. To further visualize this correlation, we plot a *Winner Map* (Figure 3) which depicts the best-performing method for each task configuration on all datasets. We can see a clear pattern showing that FOMAML is only effective when the zero-shot performance is already high, while MAMF dominates on initially more challenging tasks.

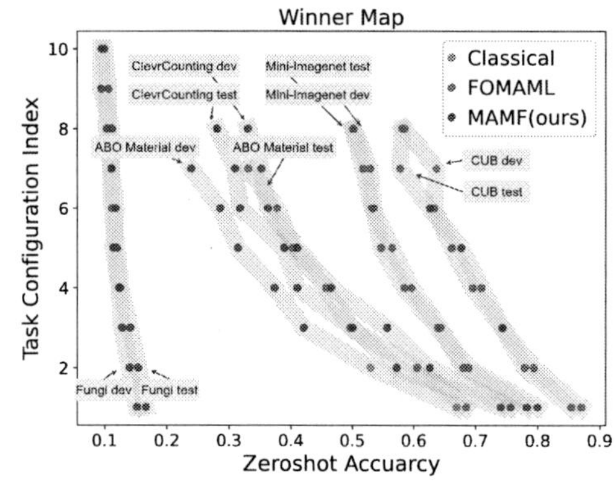

Figure 3: Each thick shaded line represents a dataset split, e.g., test set of ClevrCounting. Each dot corresponds to one task configuration in Figure 2 such as $(N = 5, T = 10)$. The color of a dot represents the best-performing algorithm. *MAMF* tends to outperform other algorithms when the problem is initially more challenging, i.e., when zero-shot accuracy is lower.

6 Conclusion

In this paper, We demonstrate the importance of *task sampling* by proposing a simple yet effective fine-tuning method MAMF. We further show novel insights on the limited effectiveness of the bi-level optimization. We hope our work encourage more research on improving few-shot transfer learning via better task sampling beyond uniform sampling.

Acknowledgements

We thank the anonymous reviewers helpful suggestions. This research is based upon work supported by U.S. DARPA AIDA Program No. FA8750-18-2-0014. The views and conclusions contained herein are those of the authors and should not be interpreted as necessarily representing the official policies, either expressed or implied, of DARPA, or the U.S. Government. The U.S. Government is authorized to reproduce and distribute reprints for governmental purposes notwithstanding any copyright annotation therein.

References

Jean-Baptiste Alayrac, Jeff Donahue, Pauline Luc, Antoine Miech, Iain Barr, Yana Hasson, Karel Lenc, Arthur Mensch, Katie Millican, Malcolm Reynolds, et al. 2022. Flamingo: a visual language model for few-shot learning. *arXiv preprint arXiv:2204.14198*.

Sébastien M R Arnold, Praateek Mahajan, Debajyoti Datta, Ian Bunner, and Konstantinos Saitas Zarkias. 2020. learn2learn: A library for Meta-Learning research.

Tom B. Brown, Benjamin Mann, Nick Ryder, Melanie Subbiah, Jared Kaplan, Prafulla Dhariwal, Arvind Neelakantan, Pranav Shyam, Girish Sastry, Amanda Askell, Sandhini Agarwal, Ariel Herbert-Voss, Gretchen Krueger, Tom Henighan, Rewon Child, Aditya Ramesh, Daniel M. Ziegler, Jeffrey Wu, Clemens Winter, Christopher Hesse, Mark Chen, Eric Sigler, Mateusz Litwin, Scott Gray, Benjamin Chess, Jack Clark, Christopher Berner, Sam McCandlish, Alec Radford, Ilya Sutskever, and Dario Amodei. 2020. Language models are few-shot learners. In *Proc. of NeurIPS*.

Ting Chen, Simon Kornblith, Mohammad Norouzi, and Geoffrey Hinton. 2020. A simple framework for contrastive learning of visual representations. In *International conference on machine learning*.

Jasmine Collins, Shubham Goel, Achleshwar Luthra, Leon Xu, Kenan Deng, Xi Zhang, Tomas F Yago Vicente, Himanshu Arora, Thomas Dideriksen, Matthieu Guillaumin, and Jitendra Malik. 2021. Abo: Dataset and benchmarks for real-world 3d object understanding. *arXiv preprint arXiv:2110.06199*.

Jacob Devlin, Ming-Wei Chang, Kenton Lee, and Kristina Toutanova. 2019. BERT: Pre-training of deep bidirectional transformers for language understanding. In *Proc. of ACL*.

Alexey Dosovitskiy, Lucas Beyer, Alexander Kolesnikov, Dirk Weissenborn, Xiaohua Zhai, Thomas Unterthiner, Mostafa Dehghani, Matthias Minderer, Georg Heigold, Sylvain Gelly, Jakob Uszkoreit, and Neil Houlsby. 2020. An image is worth 16x16 words: Transformers for image recognition at scale. In *Proc. of ICLR*.

Chelsea Finn, Pieter Abbeel, and Sergey Levine. 2017. Model-agnostic meta-learning for fast adaptation of deep networks. In *Proc. of ICML*.

Kaiming He, Xiangyu Zhang, Shaoqing Ren, and Jian Sun. 2016. Deep residual learning for image recognition. In *Proc. of CVPR*.

Chao Jia, Yinfei Yang, Ye Xia, Yi-Ting Chen, Zarana Parekh, Hieu Pham, Quoc V. Le, Yun-Hsuan Sung, Zhen Li, and Tom Duerig. 2021. Scaling up visual and vision-language representation learning with noisy text supervision. In *Proc. of ICML*.

Justin Johnson, Bharath Hariharan, Laurens Van Der Maaten, Li Fei-Fei, C Lawrence Zitnick, and Ross Girshick. 2017. Clevr: A diagnostic dataset for compositional language and elementary visual reasoning. In *Proc. of CVPR*.

Diederik P. Kingma and Jimmy Ba. 2015. Adam: A method for stochastic optimization. In *Proc. of ICLR*.

Mike Lewis, Yinhan Liu, Naman Goyal, Marjan Ghazvininejad, Abdelrahman Mohamed, Omer Levy, Veselin Stoyanov, and Luke Zettlemoyer. 2020. BART: Denoising sequence-to-sequence pre-training for natural language generation, translation, and comprehension. In *Proc. of ACL*.

Junnan Li, Dongxu Li, Caiming Xiong, and Steven Hoi. 2022. Blip: Bootstrapping language-image pre-training for unified vision-language understanding and generation. *arXiv preprint arXiv:2201.12086*.

Andreas Maurer, Massimiliano Pontil, and Bernardino Romera-Paredes. 2016. The benefit of multitask representation learning. *Proc. of JMLR*.

Alex Nichol, Joshua Achiam, and John Schulman. 2018. On first-order meta-learning algorithms. *arXiv preprint arXiv:1803.02999*.

Alec Radford, Jong Wook Kim, Chris Hallacy, Aditya Ramesh, Gabriel Goh, Sandhini Agarwal, Girish Sastry, Amanda Askell, Pamela Mishkin, Jack Clark, Gretchen Krueger, and Ilya Sutskever. 2021. Learning transferable visual models from natural language supervision. In *Proc. of ICML*.

Aniruddh Raghu, Maithra Raghu, Samy Bengio, and Oriol Vinyals. 2020. Rapid learning or feature reuse? towards understanding the effectiveness of maml. In *Proc. of ICLR*.

Aravind Rajeswaran, Chelsea Finn, Sham Kakade, and Sergey Levine. 2019. Meta-learning with implicit gradients.

Jong-Chyi Su, Zezhou Cheng, and Subhransu Maji. 2021. A realistic evaluation of semi-supervised learning for fine-grained classification. In *Proc. of CVPR*.

Sebastian Thrun and Lorien Pratt. 2012. *Learning to learn*. Springer Science & Business Media.

Nilesh Tripuraneni, Michael I. Jordan, and Chi Jin. 2020. On the theory of transfer learning: The importance of task diversity. In *Proc. of NeurIPS*.

Oriol Vinyals, Charles Blundell, Timothy Lillicrap, Daan Wierstra, et al. 2016. Matching networks for one shot learning. *Proc. of NeurIPS*.

Johannes Von Oswald, Dominic Zhao, Seijin Kobayashi, Simon Schug, Massimo Caccia, Nicolas Zucchet, and João Sacramento. 2021. Learning where to learn: Gradient sparsity in meta and continual learning. *Advances in Neural Information Processing Systems*, 34:5250–5263.

P. Welinder, S. Branson, T. Mita, C. Wah, F. Schroff, S. Belongie, and P. Perona. 2010. Caltech-UCSD Birds 200. Technical report.

Han-Jia Ye and Wei-Lun Chao. 2021. How to train your maml to excel in few-shot classification. *arXiv preprint arXiv:2106.16245*.

A Dataset Details

In this work, we compare few-shot image classification performance on five datasets representing various concepts including: ClevrCounting (Johnson et al., 2017), Amazon Berkeley Objects (ABO) (Collins et al., 2021) Material, Fungi (Su et al., 2021), Mini-Imagenet (Vinyals et al., 2016), Caltech-UCSD Birds 200 (CUB) (Welinder et al., 2010). We randomly split each dataset into disjoint training, development, and test sets, and perform subsampling to frame the experiments in a few-shot setting. Specifically, for ABO Material, we construct a subset of the original dataset by clustering images according to their Material attribute. We then manually filter out noisy samples that have multiple major materials. Table 1 shows the statistics of each dataset.

We selectively add data augmentation[2] for different datasets. By default we use *RandomResizedCrop*, *RandomHorizontalFlip* and *Normalize* for all our five datasets. We further add *ColorJitter* for Mini-Imagenet and ClevrCounting. We **disable** *ColorJitter* for CUB, Fungi, and ABO Material since the color feature is essential for doing classification on these datasets. Following the original CLIP paper (Radford et al., 2021), the input images are resized to 224×224.

[2]https://pytorch.org/vision/stable/transforms.html

Dataset	M	S^{tr}	S_A^{ts}	S_B^{ts}
ClevrCounting	10	60	10	10
Fungi	20	60	10	10
ABO Material	9	50	15	15
Mini Imagenet	10	60	10	10
CUB	10	60	10	10

Table 1: Dataset statistics. M is the total number of classes; S^{tr} is the number of training samples per class; S_A^{ts} and S_B^{ts} are the number of support set and query set samples per class during *meta-testing* respectively.

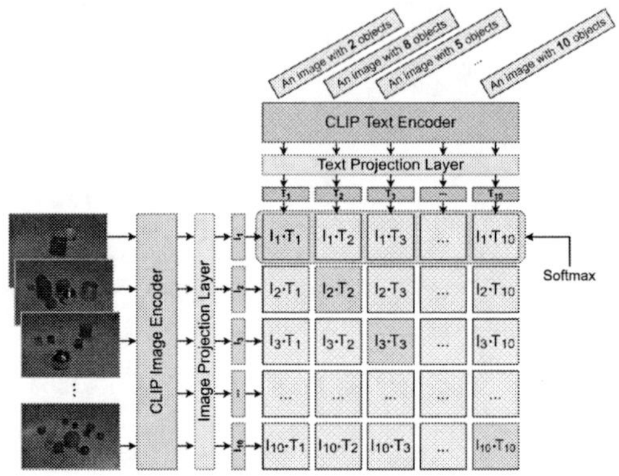

Figure 4: An illustration of the contrastive classification framework. We show a 10-way classification task on the Clevrcounting dataset. Each entry in the matrix is the similarity score (dot product) of an image embedding **I** and a text embedding **T**.

B Contrastive Image Classification Framework

We compare three algorithms (Classical Fine-tuning, MAML Fine-tuning, and MAMF) using an a contrastive classification framework based on pretrained CLIP (Radford et al., 2021). Instead of using a linear output layer mapping to N logits corresponding to N class labels, we directly compute the similarity between candidate text embeddings representing each class with the image embedding. Specifically, we create the text representation for each class by using *template prompts* filled with label names. A full list of templates we use for each dataset can be found in Table 2. Figure 4 shows an example task from the ClevrCounting dataset, where each class is represented as a string such as "An image with **2** objects". We then compute the dot product of each <image, text> embedding pairs. For each row, the label with the highest similarity score is selected as the final prediction.

Dataset	Text Input Template Example
ClevrCounting	An image of <**8**> objects.
Fungi	A photo of <**mycena pura**>.
ABO Material	An image of a product made of <**glass**>
Mini Imagenet	A photo of <**walker hound**>.
CUB	A photo of <**baltimore oriole**>.

Table 2: Example templates with filled labels for all five datasets.

C Implementation Details

We use the pretrained CLIP[3](Radford et al., 2021) with a ViT-B/32 Vision Transformer as image encoder and a masked self-attention Transformer as text encoder. The image embedding size is 768 and the text embedding size is 512. During training, we take the pre-projection image/text representation from the pretrained image/text encoder and feed them into a newly initialized[4] image/text projection layer. We choose the pre-projection representation as prior work (Chen et al., 2020) has shown that in such contrastive models the hidden layer before the last projection head serves as a better representation. Finally, we obtain an image embedding and a text embedding with the same size of 512. Note that for the Zeroshot baseline, we use the original projection layer and directly test on the query set in *meta-testing* without any fine-tuning. We train the model using cross-entropy loss for all three algorithms. We use the Adam optimizer (Kingma and Ba, 2015) with learning rate $1e-6$ during training and $1e-7$ during *meta-testing*. No weight decay is used for all algorithms during training and *meta-testing*. We use the MAML wrapper from learn2learn[5](Arnold et al., 2020) for training using first-order MAML.

D Detailed Results

Table 3 shows the detailed accuracy and standard deviation on the development sets and test sets of all the datasets shown in Figure 2 in the main paper. The (N, T) column represents the task configurations, where N stands for an N-way classification task and T stands for the total number of sampled tasks. Since the tasks are randomly sampled from the class distribution, in order to cover all classes with high probability during testing, we set the number of sampled tasks to be: $T = \frac{log(0.001)}{log(1-\frac{N}{M})}$, where M is the total number of classes. That is, with probability higher than 0.999, we can cover all classes if sampling T tasks. Columns with name *Zeroshot*, *Classical*, *MAMF*, and *FOMAML* represent models using Zeroshot CLIP, Classical Fine-tuning, Model-Agnostic Multitask Fine-tuning and first-order MAML respectively. The superscript on each accuracy percentage number indicates standard deviation across five random runs.

[3]https://huggingface.co/openai/clip-vit-base-patch32

[4]We use the Kaiming initialization implemented by Pytorch: https://pytorch.org/cppdocs/api/function_namespacetorch_1_1nn_1_1init_1ac8a913c051976a3f41f20df7d6126e57.html

[5]https://github.com/learnables/learn2learn

Table 3: Detailed average accuracy (%) and standard deviation on the development set and test set of all five datasets. The (N, T) column represents the task configurations consistent with the x-axis in Figure 3 in the main paper. Note that for the ABO Material dataset, we have 9 classes in total, so a task has up to 8-way classification. And for the Fungi dataset, which has 20 classes in total, we test on 10-way to 19-way classification tasks.

Dataset	(N, T)	Zeroshot	Classical	MAMF	FOMAML	Dataset	(N, T)	Zeroshot	Classical	MAMF	FOMAML
ABO Material Test	(2, 27)	$68.5^{2.6}$	$95.3^{1.8}$	$96.0^{1.8}$	$\mathbf{96.1}^{2.4}$	ABO Material Dev	(2, 27)	$67.0^{2.6}$	$95.2^{0.6}$	$\mathbf{94.8}^{1.2}$	$94.0^{0.4}$
	(3, 17)	$60.6^{6.0}$	$91.6^{3.0}$	$92.9^{2.4}$	$\mathbf{96.1}^{1.0}$		(3, 17)	$53.0^{1.9}$	$\mathbf{93.6}^{0.9}$	$93.2^{0.9}$	$91.7^{1.3}$
	(4, 12)	$49.6^{3.4}$	$88.6^{0.6}$	$90.1^{0.7}$	$\mathbf{94.2}^{1.6}$		(4, 12)	$42.1^{2.8}$	$89.5^{2.5}$	$\mathbf{91.3}^{2.2}$	$88.1^{1.7}$
	(5, 9)	$45.7^{1.6}$	$87.3^{1.5}$	$89.0^{1.2}$	$\mathbf{93.3}^{0.7}$		(5, 9)	$37.4^{2.6}$	$86.8^{2.2}$	$\mathbf{89.2}^{1.4}$	$89.0^{1.4}$
	(6, 6)	$40.3^{2.1}$	$82.1^{2.1}$	$86.5^{2.5}$	$\mathbf{90.5}^{1.4}$		(6, 6)	$31.5^{1.8}$	$84.4^{1.6}$	$\mathbf{88.1}^{3.2}$	$85.3^{2.9}$
	(7, 5)	$37.8^{3.4}$	$83.3^{3.0}$	$85.4^{4.0}$	$\mathbf{91.6}^{1.7}$		(7, 5)	$28.6^{2.0}$	$84.0^{1.5}$	$\mathbf{84.8}^{1.2}$	$84.2^{3.1}$
	(8, 3)	$33.2^{0.7}$	$81.3^{0.8}$	$83.6^{1.6}$	$\mathbf{89.8}^{0.9}$		(8, 3)	$23.9^{2.7}$	$80.1^{1.3}$	$\mathbf{81.9}^{1.8}$	$81.6^{1.2}$
Clevr-Counting Test	(2, 31)	$74.1^{2.2}$	$89.5^{1.7}$	$\mathbf{89.8}^{1.5}$	$85.5^{2.2}$	Clevr-Counting Dev	(2, 31)	$75.7^{3.4}$	$90.1^{2.7}$	$\mathbf{91.7}^{2.5}$	$87.3^{1.4}$
	(3, 19)	$57.3^{2.1}$	$82.5^{3.3}$	$\mathbf{83.8}^{3.8}$	$74.7^{4.5}$		(3, 19)	$62.6^{1.5}$	$81.2^{2.5}$	$\mathbf{83.6}^{3.0}$	$78.6^{4.5}$
	(4, 14)	$50.1^{2.0}$	$76.4^{2.0}$	$\mathbf{78.0}^{3.3}$	$74.1^{1.6}$		(4, 14)	$55.7^{1.9}$	$79.1^{2.0}$	$\mathbf{81.4}^{1.1}$	$73.8^{5.3}$
	(5, 10)	$41.0^{2.5}$	$67.9^{3.0}$	$\mathbf{73.0}^{2.8}$	$60.2^{9.5}$		(5, 10)	$46.6^{3.7}$	$69.7^{4.6}$	$\mathbf{71.5}^{6.1}$	$56.1^{0.9}$
	(6, 8)	$38.9^{2.6}$	$64.9^{3.9}$	$\mathbf{70.5}^{3.0}$	$64.9^{5.0}$		(6, 8)	$41.0^{1.3}$	$67.3^{2.6}$	$\mathbf{69.2}^{5.2}$	$62.0^{3.6}$
	(7, 6)	$31.9^{0.9}$	$59.4^{3.3}$	$\mathbf{64.1}^{1.7}$	$60.0^{6.9}$		(7, 6)	$36.3^{1.9}$	$59.0^{4.8}$	$\mathbf{65.0}^{4.2}$	$57.3^{1.9}$
	(8, 4)	$31.0^{1.3}$	$56.4^{5.8}$	$\mathbf{60.3}^{3.2}$	$42.9^{5.6}$		(8, 4)	$35.3^{1.2}$	$57.9^{4.6}$	$\mathbf{62.3}^{3.5}$	$42.1^{9.2}$
	(9, 3)	$28.1^{1.2}$	$56.5^{3.1}$	$\mathbf{59.7}^{4.8}$	$33.6^{13.2}$		(9, 3)	$33.1^{2.3}$	$53.2^{3.3}$	$\mathbf{53.8}^{2.6}$	$36.3^{12.6}$
CUB Test	(2, 31)	$80.0^{2.6}$	$91.2^{1.6}$	$\mathbf{96.2}^{1.8}$	$96.1^{2.9}$	CUB Dev	(2, 31)	$78.3^{1.1}$	$90.4^{1.9}$	$\mathbf{97.8}^{1.5}$	$97.5^{1.4}$
	(3, 19)	$68.9^{1.6}$	$86.1^{5.6}$	$95.1^{0.9}$	$\mathbf{97.1}^{3.3}$		(3, 19)	$68.1^{2.3}$	$88.7^{7.1}$	$96.8^{2.3}$	$\mathbf{97.5}^{2.5}$
	(4, 14)	$63.9^{3.3}$	$79.8^{4.4}$	$93.8^{2.6}$	$\mathbf{97.4}^{1.9}$		(4, 14)	$64.3^{1.9}$	$83.9^{4.6}$	$95.2^{2.8}$	$\mathbf{96.8}^{2.8}$
	(5, 10)	$58.5^{2.6}$	$77.3^{3.3}$	$85.5^{6.6}$	$\mathbf{96.4}^{1.4}$		(5, 10)	$59.7^{2.3}$	$78.9^{5.4}$	$87.0^{6.2}$	$\mathbf{97.4}^{2.2}$
	(6, 8)	$54.7^{2.0}$	$79.4^{5.5}$	$88.8^{3.0}$	$\mathbf{93.5}^{5.6}$		(6, 8)	$56.5^{1.3}$	$79.1^{0.6}$	$94.6^{3.1}$	$\mathbf{95.2}^{5.2}$
	(7, 6)	$53.5^{1.9}$	$77.0^{7.9}$	$88.3^{3.5}$	$\mathbf{98.3}^{0.3}$		(7, 6)	$53.3^{2.0}$	$77.8^{3.4}$	$88.4^{3.9}$	$98.8^{0.0}$
	(8, 4)	$52.9^{2.6}$	$71.6^{7.4}$	$80.9^{3.8}$	$\mathbf{98.1}^{0.5}$		(8, 4)	$51.8^{1.7}$	$75.0^{7.2}$	$79.9^{4.7}$	$99.4^{0.4}$
	(9, 3)	$50.2^{1.3}$	$69.9^{5.1}$	$80.7^{4.1}$	$\mathbf{98.1}^{0.7}$		(9, 3)	$50.1^{2.5}$	$64.4^{8.3}$	$80.7^{3.3}$	$\mathbf{98.8}^{0.9}$
Mini ImageNet Test	(2, 31)	$87.1^{1.4}$	$93.9^{1.5}$	$93.9^{1.5}$	$\mathbf{97.2}^{1.4}$	Mini ImageNet Dev	(2, 31)	$85.5^{2.7}$	$93.6^{0.7}$	$93.2^{3.0}$	$\mathbf{96.4}^{0.4}$
	(3, 19)	$79.4^{2.3}$	$90.0^{1.6}$	$92.3^{1.5}$	$\mathbf{93.9}^{2.6}$		(3, 19)	$78.0^{3.4}$	$89.0^{1.5}$	$91.3^{1.5}$	$\mathbf{95.6}^{0.8}$
	(4, 14)	$74.4^{3.1}$	$86.7^{1.4}$	$\mathbf{92.3}^{1.4}$	$89.9^{5.1}$		(4, 14)	$74.4^{4.2}$	$85.4^{2.4}$	$90.3^{0.7}$	$\mathbf{90.4}^{5.7}$
	(5, 10)	$71.0^{2.4}$	$86.5^{0.7}$	$\mathbf{89.2}^{1.4}$	$92.0^{0.7}$		(5, 10)	$69.6^{5.7}$	$85.7^{3.3}$	$89.0^{1.2}$	$\mathbf{93.1}^{2.6}$
	(6, 8)	$67.7^{3.4}$	$83.5^{1.1}$	$\mathbf{89.2}^{1.6}$	$86.1^{2.8}$		(6, 8)	$66.2^{2.8}$	$83.0^{1.1}$	$88.5^{1.5}$	$\mathbf{89.0}^{2.2}$
	(7, 6)	$62.6^{3.0}$	$82.3^{1.5}$	$\mathbf{89.0}^{1.3}$	$87.3^{3.1}$		(7, 6)	$63.3^{2.3}$	$78.9^{2.6}$	$86.3^{0.8}$	$\mathbf{86.8}^{2.9}$
	(8, 4)	$57.8^{1.9}$	$79.4^{2.9}$	$83.6^{3.4}$	$\mathbf{87.7}^{6.0}$		(8, 4)	$63.7^{3.2}$	$78.7^{5.0}$	$84.4^{1.7}$	$\mathbf{89.0}^{1.0}$
	(9, 3)	$58.1^{2.6}$	$78.2^{3.1}$	$82.0^{2.9}$	$\mathbf{88.7}^{1.5}$		(9, 3)	$58.5^{2.8}$	$78.2^{1.9}$	$81.5^{1.9}$	$\mathbf{86.4}^{3.1}$
Fungi Test	(10, 8)	$15.2^{0.8}$	$60.2^{1.5}$	$\mathbf{67.9}^{2.6}$	$64.7^{2.7}$	Fungi Dev	(10, 8)	$16.7^{1.4}$	$54.4^{1.1}$	$\mathbf{60.8}^{2.9}$	$58.1^{1.5}$
	(11, 8)	$14.1^{0.5}$	$57.2^{2.2}$	$\mathbf{66.3}^{1.7}$	$64.1^{1.4}$		(11, 8)	$15.4^{1.2}$	$53.9^{2.5}$	$\mathbf{60.6}^{1.0}$	$57.5^{1.5}$
	(12, 8)	$12.8^{0.7}$	$58.1^{1.9}$	$\mathbf{65.6}^{2.6}$	$61.1^{2.6}$		(12, 8)	$14.1^{0.8}$	$51.5^{3.9}$	$\mathbf{59.6}^{2.6}$	$57.6^{2.7}$
	(13, 7)	$12.4^{0.7}$	$55.8^{1.1}$	$\mathbf{64.2}^{2.7}$	$59.9^{2.3}$		(13, 7)	$12.5^{1.0}$	$49.6^{4.1}$	$\mathbf{56.0}^{1.9}$	$54.0^{1.6}$
	(14, 6)	$11.5^{1.2}$	$51.5^{2.6}$	$\mathbf{61.7}^{2.2}$	$54.1^{4.3}$		(14, 6)	$12.0^{0.6}$	$47.4^{3.3}$	$\mathbf{55.6}^{3.4}$	$53.2^{2.6}$
	(15, 5)	$11.8^{0.8}$	$53.7^{1.7}$	$\mathbf{59.2}^{3.8}$	$57.0^{1.3}$		(15, 5)	$11.2^{0.1}$	$48.6^{0.9}$	$53.9^{1.7}$	$\mathbf{54.6}^{2.8}$
	(16, 4)	$11.1^{0.5}$	$52.4^{2.6}$	$\mathbf{55.9}^{1.5}$	$53.5^{2.5}$		(16, 4)	$11.1^{0.6}$	$50.0^{3.0}$	$\mathbf{51.1}^{2.8}$	$50.3^{4.4}$
	(17, 4)	$11.2^{0.5}$	$48.8^{3.1}$	$\mathbf{54.3}^{1.4}$	$52.5^{1.0}$		(17, 4)	$10.4^{1.0}$	$44.5^{1.4}$	$\mathbf{51.2}^{2.1}$	$50.1^{1.7}$
	(18, 3)	$9.5^{0.3}$	$50.3^{3.0}$	$\mathbf{54.1}^{2.1}$	$51.5^{2.4}$		(18, 3)	$10.6^{0.3}$	$42.9^{3.1}$	$\mathbf{50.2}^{1.8}$	$45.7^{2.0}$
	(19, 2)	$9.5^{0.7}$	$48.7^{3.4}$	$\mathbf{53.1}^{3.3}$	$45.1^{2.1}$		(19, 2)	$10.0^{1.3}$	$45.8^{3.2}$	$\mathbf{47.8}^{1.6}$	$41.4^{3.0}$

Analyzing BERT Cross-lingual Transfer Capabilities in Continual Sequence Labeling

Juan M. Coria[1*] and **Mathilde Veron**[1,2*] and **Sahar Ghannay**[1]
Guillaume Bernard[2] and **Hervé Bredin**[3] and **Olivier Galibert**[2] and **Sophie Rosset**[1]

[1]Université Paris-Saclay CNRS, LISN, Orsay, France; [2]LNE, Trappes, France;
[3]IRIT, Université de Toulouse, CNRS, Toulouse, France

[1]{lastname}@lisn.fr;
[2]{name.lastname}@lne.fr; [3]{name.lastname}@irit.fr

Abstract

Knowledge transfer between neural language models is a widely used technique that has proven to improve performance in a multitude of natural language tasks, in particular with the recent rise of large pre-trained language models like BERT. Similarly, high cross-lingual transfer has been shown to occur in multilingual language models. Hence, it is of great importance to better understand this phenomenon as well as its limits. While most studies about cross-lingual transfer focus on training on independent and identically distributed (*i.e. i.i.d.*) samples, in this paper we study cross-lingual transfer in a continual learning setting on two sequence labeling tasks: slot-filling and named entity recognition. We investigate this by training multilingual BERT on sequences of 9 languages, one language at a time, on the MultiATIS++ and MultiCoNER corpora. Our first findings are that forward transfer between languages is retained although forgetting is present. Additional experiments show that lost performance can be recovered with as little as a single training epoch even if forgetting was high, which can be explained by a progressive shift of model parameters towards a better multilingual initialization. We also find that commonly used metrics might be insufficient to assess continual learning performance.

1 Introduction

State-of-the-art models for Natural Language Processing (NLP) usually leverage deep neural networks. In particular, pre-trained Transformer-based (Vaswani et al., 2017) language models like BERT (Devlin et al., 2019) have proven to perform very well on various NLP tasks, often achieving state-of-the-art results (Raffel et al., 2020; Brown et al., 2020). These models are pre-trained in a self-supervised way on large text corpora and rely on knowledge transfer to solve downstream tasks, where the pre-trained model is fine-tuned on the target task. Multilingual versions of these models have also been trained and demonstrate high cross-lingual transfer as well (K et al., 2020; Wang et al., 2020; Conneau et al., 2020; Xue et al., 2020). Given the interest in these models for cross-lingual transfer, it is of great importance to better understand this phenomenon as well as its limits.

In this work, we analyse the cross-lingual transfer capabilities of multilingual BERT and we work on sequence labeling, where each token of a sentence must be annotated with a specific label. This problem regroups various NLP tasks like Named Entity Recognition (NER), Part-Of-Speech (POS) Tagging, text chunking and slot-filling. We focus our study on two of these tasks using two multilingual corpora[1]: MultiATIS++ for slot-filling (Xu et al., 2020) and MultiCoNER for NER (Malmasi et al., 2022a,b). Experimenting on different corpora allows us to identify which observations may generalize and which ones may be corpus specific.

While most cross-lingual transfer studies about slot-filling or NER focus either on joint training or training on a source and a target language (Xu et al., 2020; Schuster et al., 2019; Arkhipov et al., 2019; Mueller et al., 2020; Wang et al., 2020), our main contribution is a study with special focus on *continual* cross-lingual transfer, where the model performs one single task but is progressively adapted over a sequence of languages.

We believe this experimental setup to be interesting not only as a novel way of studying cross-lingual transfer but also because it is better suited to real case scenarios. Indeed, adaptation to new data over time is a highly desirable feature of most NLP models: oftentimes, collecting data and an-

*These authors have contributed equally. The order is alphabetical.

[1]We do not work on the recent MASSIVE (FitzGerald et al., 2022) corpus as we consider it too similar to MultiATIS++. We also avoid Universal Depedencies (Nivre et al., 2020) because we consider POS tagging to be too simple for this type of study. Moreover, the amount of per-language data in the latter could bias the transfer we observe.

Proceedings of the 29th International Conference on Computational Linguistics, pages 15–25
October 12–17, 2022.

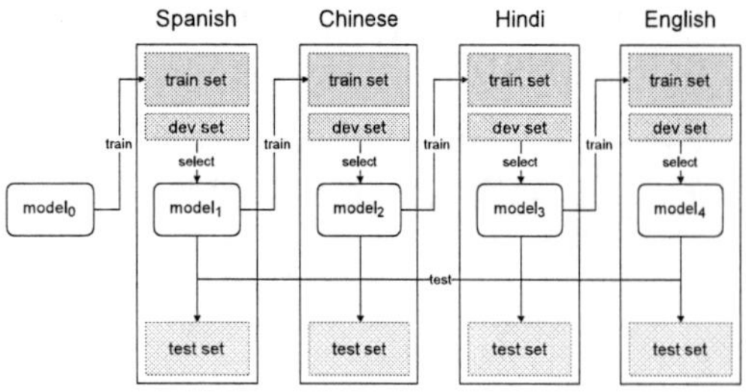

Figure 1: Depiction of a training sequence across 4 languages. For each language in the given order, we train the model on its training set, select the best epoch on the development set and then test on all test sets independently.

Language	Utterances *train*	*dev*	*test*	Labels
MultiATIS++				
Hindi	1,440	160	893	75
Turkish	578	60	715	71
Others	4,488	490	893	84
MultiCoNER				
All	15,3K	800	≥138K	6

Table 1: Number of sentences per subset and number of unique labels (without B and I prefix) for each language in MultiATIS++ (Xu et al., 2020) and MultiCoNER (Malmasi et al., 2022a).

notating them is expensive, which makes training data scarce or incomplete at the beginning of a project. Additionally, model requirements might also evolve with time based on the needs of the users. This means that the model has to adapt sequentially as training data becomes available. An example of this could be a dialogue system that is gradually deployed in different countries. Unfortunately, naive solutions to adapt a previously trained model are costly, as they require either re-training from scratch or maintaining many distinct models.

On the other hand, progressively training on multiple datasets that become available one by one is at the heart of continual learning (Hadsell et al., 2020), where the goal is for a model to improve itself both on past and new data. We refer to these datasets and the order in which they appear as a *training sequence* (f.i. see Figure 1). Traditional training schemes assume that training examples (in our case annotated sentences) are independent and identically distributed (*i.i.d.*), which does not usually hold when data becomes available sequentially. Moreover, access to previous data is not allowed[2], as this represents a linear use of resources with respect to the length of the sequence, which can in theory be infinite. In this context, transfer is generally divided in two: forward and backward (Hadsell et al., 2020; Lopez-Paz and Ranzato, 2017; Arora et al., 2019), defined in our case as improvement on future and already acquired languages respectively. The biggest challenge of continual learning systems is catastrophic forgetting (Hadsell et al., 2020; French, 1999), which is defined as a strong performance loss in previously acquired knowledge (*i.e.* negative backward transfer). While previous studies on continual learning tend to focus on the domain axis for the slot-filling task (Lee, 2017; Madotto et al., 2020), or on the class axis for the NER task (Monaikul et al., 2021; Xia et al., 2022), we concentrate on the axis of language adaptation.

Similar work also investigates cross-lingual transfer of multilingual BERT fine-tuned on sequence labeling tasks, namely NER and POS-Tagging (Liu et al., 2021). They focus on preserving masked language modeling performance and cross-lingual ability after fine-tuning on one of the two tasks on English only, with a method developed as part of continual learning. Conversely, our work focuses on fine-tuning on a single task over a sequence of many languages.

In this paper, we first describe in Section 2 and 3 the task, the corpora and the model we are working with. Then in Section 4 we define the different continual learning metrics that we use in our experiment. Our study is guided by the following research questions, as presented in Section 5: does cross-lingual transfer exist during continual training or does catastrophic forgetting prevent it? How much transfer can we expect relative to monolingual and multilingual *i.i.d.* training? In Section 6 we perform an extensive analysis on MultiATIS++ in order to understand how transfer is affected by the training sequence. Finally, in Section 7 we investigate whether lost performance (due to forgetting) can be recovered and at what cost.

2 Task and corpora

2.1 Sequence labeling

In sequence labeling, each token of a sentence must be annotated with a specific label. Hence, it is appropriate to identify concepts or entities in sen-

[2]Access to previous data is sometimes allowed if limited (Robins, 1995)

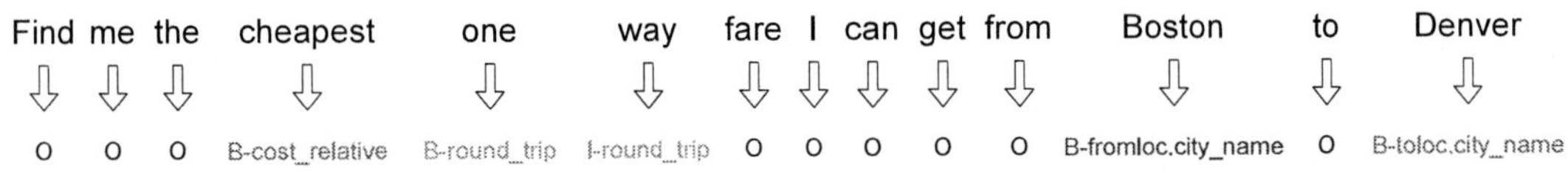

Figure 2: Example of slot filling IOB (Ramshaw and Marcus, 1995) labels for an utterance of MultiATIS++ (Xu et al., 2020) in English. Label "O" (from *outside*) denotes that no concept is mentioned, "B" (from *beginning*) denotes the first word of a concept and "I" (from *inside*) the continuation of a concept. Different slot types are shown in different colors.

tences. In our case, the labels to predict are the same across languages so that the task remains unchanged over the continual learning process.

Sequences are labeled using the IOB format (Ramshaw and Marcus, 1995), where labels consist of a prefix (B,I or O) and an optional type that categorizes the identified concept. While O indicates that the token is not part of a concept (O for outside), B and I indicate that it is the beginning or continuation of a concept, thus allowing the identification of multi-token concepts. An example of this labeling scheme is shown in Figure 2.

This task is usually evaluated using the slot micro F1 score (Tjong Kim Sang and Buchholz, 2000).

2.2 MultiATIS++

The MultiATIS++ multilingual corpus comes from the Air Travel Information System (ATIS) corpus (Hemphill et al., 1990), consisting in utterances of users asking for flight information. The corpus focuses on the slot-filling task, which is related to task-oriented dialogue systems. It enables the system to identify the important concepts mentioned by the user that are needed to successfully continue the dialogue. These concepts are related to the system's domain and to the tasks that the system should perform. This corpus is the manual translation of the original English (EN) ATIS sentences into 6 different languages: Spanish (ES), Portuguese (PT), German (DE), French (FR), Chinese (ZH) and Japanese (JA). It also includes two additional languages: Hindi (HI) and Turkish (TR), that were added as part of MultiATIS in (Upadhyay et al., 2018).

Contrary to the translations added in MultiATIS++, the number of utterances of Hindi and Turkish translations are not as many as for the other languages. More details on the composition of MultiATIS++ are shown in Table 1.

2.3 MultiCoNER

The MultiCoNER corpus was proposed as part of the SemEval 2022 Task 11 (Malmasi et al., 2022a,b) and focuses on the NER task. While it is usually a generic task consisting in identifying entities like people, organizations, locations or dates in written texts, this corpus focuses on detecting ambiguous and complex entities in short and low-context settings. These entities are person, location, group, corporation, product and creative work. MultiCoNER also aims at stimulating the research on multilingual models, as it contains annotations in 11 languages. For a fair comparison with MultiATIS++, we restrict these experiments to also contain 9 languages, namely Bengali (BN), German (DE), English (EN), Spanish (ES), Hindi (HI), Korean (KO), Dutch (NL), Turkish (TR) and Chinese (ZH). More details on the composition of MultiCoNER are shown in Table 1. In the rest of the paper and for both corpora we denote the *train*, *dev* and *test* sets of a given language i with a subscript (e.g. $train_i$).

3 Model

We use the multilingual BERT (Devlin et al., 2019) base model, consisting of 12 multi-head attention layers with 12 heads and hidden size of 768 (177M parameters). This model was trained on large Wikipedia dumps from 104 different languages using masked language modelling and next sentence prediction objectives.

As we use the model for sequence labeling, we append a two-layer feed-forward classifier with hidden size 768 and ReLU (rectified linear unit) activation (Nair and Hinton, 2010). The input of the classifier are the last layer word hidden states after applying dropout with $p = 0.1$.

Following (Xu et al., 2020), we train the model on MultiATIS++ using the Adam optimizer (Kingma and Ba, 2015) with a learning rate of 10^{-5} and a batch size of 32 utterances for

50 epochs (unless stated otherwise), selecting the model with the highest slot F1 on the corresponding *dev* set. We train the model on MultiCoNER the same way, except for the learning rate (optimized on *dev* and set to 5×10^{-5}) and the number of epochs, which is set to 15. We evaluate the model on all $test_i$ sets for every language i using the slot F1 calculated with the `seqeval` library (Nakayama, 2018).

4 Continual Learning Metrics

Cross-lingual transfer can be defined as the performance improvement of a model on a particular language based on knowledge of other languages. This can take several forms depending on the training structure. In an *i.i.d.* context, where all data are available from the start, we think of transfer in terms of joint training. If training on language i and j jointly (multilingual) yields better performance on j than training only on j (monolingual), then there is transfer from i to j.

However, continual learning adds a different dimension. Indeed, when training on a language sequence we can identify two types of transfer: forwards and backwards (Hadsell et al., 2020; Lopez-Paz and Ranzato, 2017). Forward transfer denotes the performance and learning efficiency improvement on a given language thanks to previously acquired knowledge of other languages. Conversely, backward transfer denotes the performance improvement on a previously acquired language when learning a new one. More formally, and similarly to Lopez-Paz and Ranzato (2017), given a sequence of L languages, we define the performance matrix $P \in \mathbb{R}^{L \times L}$, where P_{ij} is the performance of language i after learning language j. In this context, backward transfer of i is defined as:

$$\mathrm{BT}_i = P_{iL} - P_{ii} \tag{1}$$

Negative backward transfer is also called forgetting, as it denotes performance loss on previous languages. Since P_{11} is equivalent to monolingual performance mono_1, we can define backward transfer of the first language after learning language j:

$$\mathrm{BT}_{1j} = P_{1j} - \mathrm{mono}_1 \tag{2}$$

Conversely, we define forward transfer as:

$$\mathrm{FT}_i^{\mathrm{mono}} = P_{ii} - \mathrm{mono}_i \tag{3}$$

where mono_i denotes monolingual performance on language i. By comparing performance with a different baseline like multilingual, we can measure how close forward transfer is to joint transfer:

$$\mathrm{FT}_i^{\mathrm{multi}} = P_{ii} - \mathrm{multi}_i \tag{4}$$

where multi_i denotes the multilingual performance on language i. These definitions will be useful for the analysis in Section 6.

5 Cross-lingual Transfer

Does transfer exist during continual training or does catastrophic forgetting prevent it?

Before studying the continual learning scenario, we first measure transfer when training the model on all languages at once (*i.e. joint* transfer). Then, having this frame of reference, we investigate transfer when training the model on each language sequentially (*i.e. continual* transfer).

5.1 Joint Transfer

In order to measure transfer in unstructured *i.i.d.* training, we train the model on all languages together (multilingual) and compare the performance we obtain with monolingual training. Note that multilingual training corresponds to concatenating all $train_i$ for training and all dev_i for validation. We report the mean and standard deviation of *test* slot F1 per language across 5 runs to reduce the effect of randomness.

Results on MultiATIS++ are reported in Table 2. We observe that multilingual is always stronger than monolingual (except for Chinese and Japanese), which confirms the existence of joint cross-lingual transfer. European languages (German, English, Spanish, French and Portuguese) show modest but visible gains from transfer, whereas Asian languages (Chinese and Japanese) do not seem to benefit from it. However, transfer for the two low resource languages (Hindi and Turkish) is outstanding, with an absolute 4.8% and 13.9% improvement. As noted in (Do et al., 2020), MultiATIS++ translations keep the same (unrealistic) slot values for particular labels (e.g. American *departure city* and *destination city* in Turkish utterances). We suspect this may be the reason why transfer is particularly high in this corpus. The fact that the corpus contains less training data for Hindi and Turkish than for the other languages might also

Training	DE	EN	ES	FR	PT	ZH	JA	HI	TR	Model Cost		Data Cost
										Time	Space	Space
Monolingual	94.4 (0.2)	95.6 (0.1)	88.9 (0.4)	93.2 (0.1)	90.3 (0.6)	93.3 (0.4)	93.1 (0.4)	82.4 (0.5)	71.3 (0.9)	≤224K	1.6B	≤4K
Multilingual	95.0 (0.2)	96.0 (0.2)	90.4 (0.4)	94.0 (0.3)	91.4 (0.2)	93.6 (0.2)	93.0 (0.1)	87.2 (0.3)	85.2 (0.6)	1.7M	178M	33K
Joint transfer	+0.6	+0.4	+1.5	+0.8	+1.1	+0.3	-0.1	+4.8	+13.9	-	-	-
Continual (P_{LL})	94.9 (0.2)	95.9 (0.1)	89.9 (0.5)	93.9 (0.3)	91.3 (0.3)	93.9 (0.3)	93.1 (0.3)	85.6 (0.7)	84.0 (0.6)	≤224K	178M	≤4K
FT_{1L}^{mono}	+0.5	+0.3	+1.0	+0.7	+1.0	+0.6	+0.0	+3.2	+12.7	-	-	-
Continual (P_{1L})	94.0 (0.7)	95.5 (0.2)	89.2 (0.5)	91.4 (1.7)	88.4 (4.9)	92.0 (1.0)	91.7 (0.7)	80.5 (1.8)	68.1 (3.5)	≤224K	178M	≤4K
BT_{1L}	-0.4	-0.1	+0.3	-1.8	-1.9	-1.3	-1.4	-1.9	-3.2	-	-	-

Table 2: Slot F1 performance on MultiATIS++ on $test_i$ sets for monolingual, multilingual and continual experiments. The latter are calculated as the average of the first (P_{1L}) or last (P_{LL}) language (indicated by the column) at the end of the sequence. See Equations 2 and 3 for the definition of BT_{1L} and FT_{1L}^{mono}. Reported values are the average of 5 runs with standard deviation shown in parenthesis. Model time cost denotes the cost of adding a new language to the model measured in iterations. Model space cost is the size of the model measured in number of parameters. Data space cost represents the maximum number of training sentences stored in memory at the same time.

Training	BN	DE	EN	ES	HI	KO	NL	TR	ZH	Model Cost		Data Cost
										Time	Space	Space
Monolingual	41.6 (3.2)	64.1 (0.8)	61.3 (0.6)	59.0 (0.8)	43.1 (1.2)	56.7 (0.7)	61.4 (0.9)	45.7 (0.7)	57.6 (0.8)	765K	1.6B	15K
Multilingual	44.9 (1.6)	66.9 (0.4)	64.4 (0.7)	63.8 (0.4)	46.4 (1.2)	59.4 (0.8)	66.5 (0.5)	50.6 (1.0)	58.2 (1.0)	6.9M	178M	138K
Joint transfer	+3.3	+2.8	+3.1	+4.8	+3.3	+2.7	+5.1	+4.9	+0.6	-	-	-
Continual (P_{LL})	43.4 (1.8)	66.0 (0.6)	63.0 (0.6)	62.1 (0.9)	44.2 (1.0)	57.0 (0.7)	64.6 (0.6)	50.1 (0.8)	56.2 (1.3)	765K	178M	15K
FT_{1L}^{mono}	+1.8	+1.9	+1.7	+3.1	+1.1	+0.3	+3.2	+4.4	-1.4	-	-	-
Continual (P_{1L})	31.7 (4.5)	50.9 (1.5)	52.5 (2.6)	51.1 (2.3)	32.2 (2.4)	43.2 (2.4)	55.4 (3.4)	37.4 (1.9)	40.0 (2.8)	765K	178M	15K
BT_{1L}	-9.9	-13.2	-8.8	-7.9	-10.9	-13.6	-6.0	-8.3	-17.6	-	-	-

Table 3: Slot F1 performance on MultiCoNER on $test_i$ sets for monolingual, multilingual and continual experiments. Same comments from Table 2 apply.

explain why joint transfer is much higher for these two languages.

Table 3 shows results on MultiCoNER. Monolingual results are much lower than in MultiATIS++ even if the number of labels to predict is much lower, suggesting that MultiCoNER is more difficult than MultiATIS++. Although the corpus is not parallel, we observe significant joint cross-lingual transfer (except for Chinese where it is negligible). This is somehow surprising considering that only a maximum of 8% of entity mentions appearing in the test set of a given language are common to those appearing in the train set of other languages.

However, multilingual training assumes that all languages are available at once. As mentioned before, this is not always true in practice, since utterances may be scarce and annotations expensive. Moreover, given N the maximum number of utterances per language and L the number of languages, training on a new language has time cost $O(LN)$, as the whole model needs to be trained from scratch. A naive solution is to use multiple monolingual models, raising however the space cost to $O(LN)$. Reducing both costs to $O(N)$ motivates our decision to structure training as a sequence.

5.2 Continual Transfer

Given a training sequence (a list of languages in a given order), continual learning consists in training the model on $train_i$ (and validating on dev_i) for each language i in the given order, as depicted in Figure 1. Although having all languages at once is not required and the language addition cost is the lowest, this approach is prone to forgetting previously learned languages.

In the experiments of this section, we report for both forward and backward transfer the average performance per language. The experiments consist of 3 sequences per language and per transfer type repeated 5 times to reduce the effect of randomness, making a total of 54 sequences and 270 experiments. These 3 sequences per language are chosen randomly and maximizing the Kendall rank correlation coefficient (Abdi, 2007) as a distance criterion so that they are as dissimilar as possible.

We first investigate whether forward transfer exists in continual training by looking at the average P_{LL} performance (*e.g.* model$_4$ evaluated on English in Figure 1) against monolingual and multilingual. Notice that we look at the performance of the last language, as this allows us to measure whether the model leverages past knowledge to learn a new language. This has the advantage of isolating the effect of forward transfer from that of backward transfer. When generating the sequences we also make sure that each language appears at the *end* of the sequence the same number of times.

Similarly, we look at backward transfer by comparing the average P_{1L} performance (*e.g.* model$_4$ evaluated on Spanish in Figure 1) against monolingual, making sure that each language appears at the *beginning* of the sequence the same number of times. This way we can determine whether the initial performance (equal to monolingual) improves with the introduction of new languages to the model. We also look at the performance of the first language, so that the effect of backward transfer is isolated from that of forward transfer.

Notice that whether we focus on the first or the last language, we always look at the performance at the end of the training sequence so that the comparison to multilingual is fair.

Results on MultiATIS++ are reported in Table 2. We observe that continual training benefits from cross-lingual forward transfer. Indeed, P_{LL} is on average closer to multilingual than to monolingual performance. However, although transfer is present for the last language, P_{1L} suffers from the opposite effect, even falling under monolingual performance. Our results show that contrary to what we expected from the identical slot values of MultiATIS++ (e.g. American *departure city* and *destination city* in Turkish utterances), the naturally occurring cross-lingual transfer completely vanishes in previous languages.

Similar observations can be made from MultiCoNER continual experiments from Table 3. Although forward transfer is high in general, it is also lower than the standard deviation for Bengali, Hindi and Korean, and even negative for Chinese. The negative backward transfer values also show that the model forgets a lot about the first language it learnt.

Overall we can see that continual training benefits from forward transfer, although still not performing as well as the multilingual topline, whereas forgetting is clearly present.

6 Training Sequence

How is transfer affected by the training sequence?

In order to better understand the effect of the training sequence on transfer, we first look at measures of forward transfer at each position relative to monolingual and multilingual. Secondly, we study the impact of the training sequence length on backward transfer measured on the first language. This analysis is conducted only on MultiATIS++ due to time and computational constraints. In the figures of this section, the mean, median and percentiles do take into account eventual outlier languages, while the minimum and maximum do not.

When considering forward transfer, Figure 3a shows that apart from the first position (equal to monolingual), the model consistently benefits from transfer at any point in the sequence, as performance is higher than monolingual. Interestingly, due to some outlier languages (generally Hindi and Turkish), we observe that the means are poor estimates of the distribution when measuring $\text{FT}_i^{\text{mono}}$. This is an indicator that commonly used continual transfer metrics might over- or underestimate real performance when transfer is not uniformly distributed among languages. Indeed, these metrics usually consist of averages across the adaptation axis (Lopez-Paz and Ranzato, 2017). In Figure 3b, we also observe that performance gets closer to multilingual as the sequence advances, although it rarely outperforms it.

As per backward transfer, Figure 4 shows that performance of the first language is in general worse than monolingual for any given sequence length. In particular, we observe that performance loss is not strictly monotonic, which means that measuring forgetting between the beginning and the end of the sequence may not be sufficient to explain how the model forgets. Note that a sequence of $L = 7$ would have shown less forgetting than a sequence of $L = 5$.

Furthermore, as hinted by continual experiments from Table 2, we observe that backward transfer deteriorates as forward transfer improves with the length of the sequence. Since negative backward transfer (*i.e.* forgetting) tends to be linked to a loss of previously acquired knowledge, it is surprising that new language performance keeps increasing while performance of known languages decreases. Our results indicate that the preserved knowledge that facilitates the acquisition of a new language in multilingual BERT for slot filling is not the same knowledge that preserves previous language performance. This might be explained by a progressive shift of model parameters towards a better multilingual initialization for the ATIS task that might however fail to retain the specificities of previous

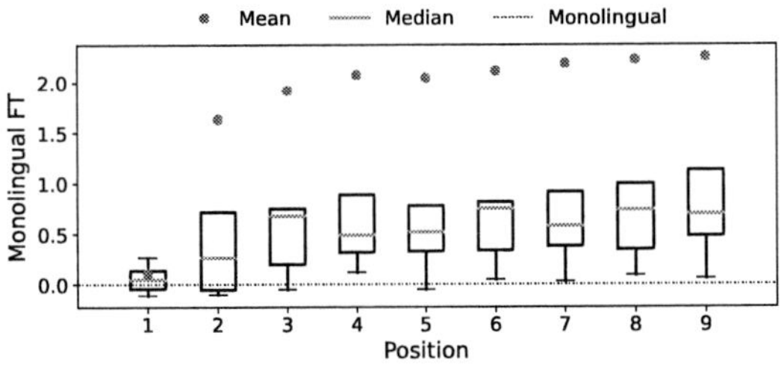

(a) $\mathrm{FT}_i^{\mathrm{mono}} = P_{ii} - \mathrm{mono}_i$ (higher is better)

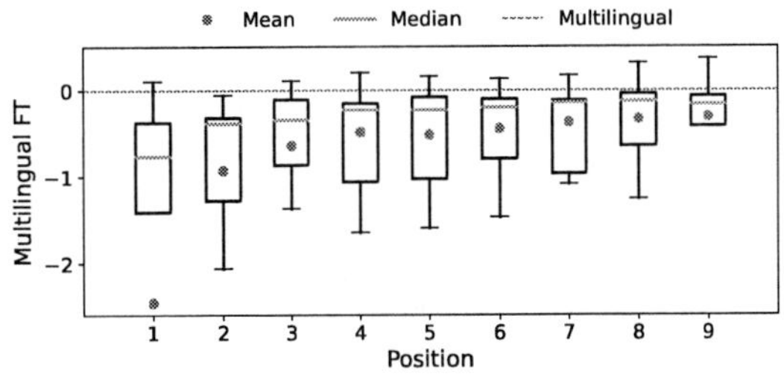

(b) $\mathrm{FT}_i^{\mathrm{multi}} = P_{ii} - \mathrm{multi}_i$ (higher is better)

Figure 3: Distributions of forward transfer on *test*$_i$ relative to monolingual and multilingual for different positions i in the sequence. We average over 54 sequences and 5 runs. Note that forward transfer is 0 when performance is equal to (a) monolingual and (b) multilingual. Outliers not shown for readability.

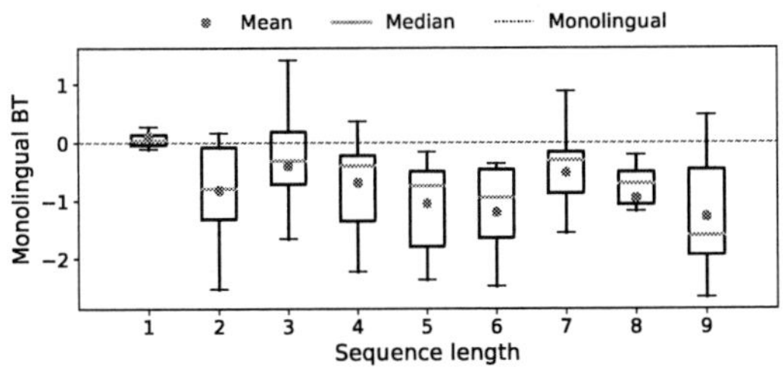

Figure 4: Distributions of first language backward transfer $\mathrm{BT}_{1j} = P_{1j} - \mathrm{mono}_1$ (higher is better) on *test*$_1$ for different sequence lengths j. We average across 54 sequences and 5 runs. Note that $\mathrm{BT}_{1j} = 0$ if performance is equal to monolingual. Outliers not shown for readability.

languages. This hypothesis motivates our next research question.

7 Fast Recovery

Can lost performance due to forgetting be recovered?

Given that forward transfer does not seem to be affected by forgetting, we investigate in this section whether performance lost as a result of forgetting can be recovered quickly after continual training. The ability to recover is especially interesting for MultiCoNER where forgetting is pretty high, but we still conduct experiments on both corpora. To investigate if this is possible, we first set out to discover whether the model shifts towards a better multilingual initialization. Hence we compare the multilingual performance of the initial model_0 (consisting of BERT and a random classifier) against model_L, the model at the end of training sequence (*e.g.* model_4 in Figure 1). In particular, we train both models on all languages jointly for different numbers of epochs and evaluate on each language. Notice that model_L comes from our continual P_{1L} experiments (see Table 2). The results are presented in Tables 4 and 5.

The comparison between model_0 multilingual and model_L multilingual for both corpora shows two interesting results. On one hand, we observe that even one epoch of multilingual training for model_L achieves better performance than the monolingual baseline (model_0 monolingual) and is even close to the multilingual topline (model_0 multilingual)[3], both of which are trained on the maximum number of epochs (50 or 15). This means that model_L is capable of achieving good multilingual performance with very little training, hence canceling the effect of forgetting. On the other hand, we see that model_L multilingual performance is greatly superior to model_0 multilingual with a single training epoch. This is not surprising given that the classifier is initialized randomly in model_0, but it shows that the model is capable of retaining knowledge from previous languages, although it is not clear whether that knowledge is preserved in the classifier or in BERT.

We dive deeper into this question by training model_L with a random classifier in the same manner (see model_L + rnd clf multi. in Table 4). We observe that performance is still greatly superior to model_0 multilingual with a single epoch. However, performance is not as high as model_L multilingual (although slightly in MultiCoNER), which keeps its continually trained classifier. This indicates most of the knowledge retained from previous languages is stored in BERT, and that the knowledge stored

[3] Except for Chinese on MultiCoNER, which is not surprising considering that its joint transfer is negligible.

Model	Epochs	DE	EN	ES	FR	PT	ZH	JA	HI	TR
model_0 multi. (*i.i.d.*)	1	82.7 (1.2)	83.6 (0.7)	78.2 (0.3)	80.7 (0.7)	79.4 (0.5)	83.5 (0.7)	82.7 (1.0)	79.6 (0.7)	69.8 (1.5)
	5	94.7 (0.2)	95.3 (0.2)	89.9 (0.2)	93.2 (0.2)	90.7 (0.2)	94.0 (0.2)	93.2 (0.5)	85.9 (0.3)	83.6 (0.7)
	50	95.0 (0.2)	96.0 (0.2)	90.4 (0.4)	94.0 (0.3)	91.4 (0.2)	93.6 (0.2)	93.0 (0.1)	87.2 (0.3)	85.2 (0.6)
model_L multi.	1	94.8 (0.3)	95.9 (0.2)	89.7 (0.6)	93.8 (0.3)	91.2 (0.4)	93.6 (0.5)	93.3 (0.3)	85.7 (0.9)	82.8 (1.3)
	5	94.9 (0.2)	95.9 (0.2)	90.0 (0.5)	93.9 (0.3)	91.3 (0.4)	93.7 (0.4)	93.3 (0.3)	86.0 (0.8)	83.4 (1.0)
model_L + rnd clf multi.	1	93.1 (0.5)	93.7 (0.5)	87.9 (0.5)	91.1 (0.5)	88.5 (0.6)	92.6 (0.5)	92.3 (0.6)	83.4 (0.8)	80.8 (1.3)
	5	94.8 (0.2)	95.8 (0.2)	89.9 (0.5)	93.6 (0.3)	91.1 (0.4)	93.7 (0.4)	93.3 (0.3)	86.3 (0.6)	84.1 (0.8)
model_0 mono. (*i.i.d.*)	50	94.4 (0.2)	95.6 (0.1)	88.9 (0.4)	93.2 (0.1)	90.3 (0.6)	93.3 (0.4)	93.1 (0.4)	82.4 (0.5)	71.3 (0.9)
model_L mono.	1	95.1 (0.2)	95.8 (0.2)	90.2 (0.4)	93.6 (0.4)	91.2 (0.4)	93.5 (0.5)	93.4 (0.2)	86.3 (0.6)	79.1 (1.5)
	5	95.0 (0.2)	95.8 (0.2)	90.0 (0.4)	94.0 (0.2)	91.3 (0.2)	93.8 (0.4)	93.4 (0.2)	86.7 (0.4)	81.6 (0.8)
	10	95.1 (0.2)	95.8 (0.2)	90.0 (0.5)	93.9 (0.3)	91.3 (0.4)	93.8 (0.4)	93.4 (0.2)	86.7 (0.4)	82.2 (0.9)

Table 4: Slot F1 performance on $test_i$ sets for MultiATIS++ fast recovery experiments. model_L monolingual performance is averaged over 3 sequences (the P_{1L} experiment ones starting with the language in question), while model_L multilingual is averaged over all 27 sequences from P_{1L} experiments. Both model_0 and model_L experiments are averaged over 5 runs (standard deviation in parenthesis).

Model	Epochs	BN	DE	EN	ES	HI	KO	NL	TR	ZH
model_0 multi. (*i.i.d.*)	1	36.2 (1.4)	63.1 (0.8)	61.6 (0.6)	60.5 (0.6)	40.5 (1.4)	56.9 (0.4)	63.5 (0.7)	45.5 (0.6)	53.1 (2.4)
	5	43.0 (1.1)	66.6 (1.0)	63.9 (0.2)	63.7 (0.6)	45.4 (1.5)	58.9 (0.7)	66.3 (0.7)	49.7 (1.4)	57.7 (1.5)
	15	44.9 (1.6)	66.9 (0.4)	64.4 (0.7)	63.8 (0.4)	46.4 (1.2)	59.4 (0.8)	66.5 (0.5)	50.6 (1.0)	58.2 (1.0)
model_L multi. (*i.i.d.*)	1	42.7 (1.7)	65.8 (0.7)	63.6 (0.7)	63.0 (0.8)	44.8 (1.4)	58.8 (1.0)	65.9 (0.8)	49.8 (1.0)	56.7 (1.3)
	5	43.8 (1.4)	66.4 (0.6)	64.1 (0.5)	63.5 (0.6)	45.4 (1.1)	59.2 (0.8)	66.4 (0.5)	50.6 (0.9)	57.6 (1.2)
model_L + rnd clf multi.	1	42.6 (1.8)	65.5 (0.7)	63.3 (0.6)	62.7 (0.8)	44.7 (1.3)	58.7 (0.8)	65.7 (0.7)	49.6 (1.2)	56.6 (1.4)
	5	43.7 (1.4)	66.3 (0.6)	63.9 (0.6)	63.4 (0.7)	45.2 (1.1)	59.1 (0.8)	66.2 (0.6)	50.4 (1.0)	57.6 (1.1)
model_0 mono. (*i.i.d.*)	15	41.6 (3.2)	64.1 (0.8)	61.3 (0.6)	59.0 (0.8)	43.1 (1.2)	56.7 (0.7)	61.4 (0.9)	45.7 (0.7)	57.6 (0.8)
model_L mono.	1	41.8 (2.4)	65.5 (0.7)	63.7 (0.8)	61.6 (0.5)	44.2 (1.1)	57.6 (0.4)	64.6 (0.7)	49.5 (1.0)	56.0 (0.9)
	5	43.6 (1.8)	66.5 (0.5)	64.0 (0.6)	62.4 (0.6)	45.4 (0.7)	57.9 (0.5)	65.0 (0.8)	50.7 (0.7)	58.3 (0.9)

Table 5: Slot F1 performance on $test_i$ sets for MultiCoNER fast recovery experiments. Same comments from Table 4 apply.

in the classifier is dependent on the corpus.

Overall, these results lead us to think that for the sequence labeling task, continual training over the language sequence does indeed shift model parameters to a better multilingual initialization. As a result, we explore the possibility to leverage this phenomenon in order to quickly recover lost language specificities due to forgetting for both corpora. To do this, we train model_L on the first language of the sequence a second time (*i.e.* as if it were an $(L+1)^{\text{th}}$ language) and evaluate on the first language only. As shown in Tables 4 and 5, when comparing model_L monolingual to model_0 monolingual (equal to first language performance P_{11}), we see that the performance of the first language can be recovered and improved upon with as little as a single training epoch[3]. These results are outstanding for MultiCoNER considering the high forgetting that we previously observed. On MultiATIS++, model_L monolingual even achieves 50-epoch model_0 multilingual performance in most cases after only one epoch, with the remaining languages still showing a big improvement. In particular, Hindi and Turkish improve an absolute 3.9% and 7.8% from model_0 monolingual respectively.

Note that for MultiATIS++ increasing the number of recovery epochs for the first language does not bring considerable improvements. The only exception to this observation is Turkish, which might be explained by the small size of its training set. In MultiCoNER however, performance still improves after 5 epochs, getting closer to the multilingual topline. Surprisingly, model_L monolingual is even on par with the multilingual topline for Turkish and Chinese. Although the cost of adding a language remains $O(N)$, the ability to recover all languages raises costs to $O(LN)$, making it expensive to use in practice. The design of a strategy taking full advantage of these recovery capabilities to limit forgetting with lower cost is left for future work.

8 Discussion

To summarize, we observe a high level of cross-lingual transfer in the *i.i.d.* setting when learning the sequence labeling task on all languages jointly for both corpora. In a real low resource scenario where data and annotations are scarce, it may be difficult or even impossible to implement either a monolingual or multilingual adaptive approach, as time/space complexity is high and not all languages might be available at once. In a continual learning setting where languages are learned in sequence, these costs are the lowest and cross-lingual transfer is retained in the form of forward transfer. However, forgetting occurs for the first language of the sequence since performance consistently drops below monolingual.

When looking at continual cross-lingual transfer across the entire sequence, we obtain two surprising results. First, commonly used continual transfer metrics may not be a reliable estimate of the performance distribution across languages when transfer is not evenly distributed. Since even in other adaptation axes a considerable variability across datasets is to be expected, we believe a statistic like the median might be a better choice, as we believe it better represents expected performance at any given point. Second, as the sequence progresses, forward transfer improves, while backward transfer diminishes. This might indicate that model parameters remain a good initialization for future languages but that previous language specificities might be lost.

Motivated by this hypothesis, we compare the model at the beginning and at the end of the training sequence. Our results suggest that knowledge from past languages is mostly stored in BERT (as opposed to the task-specific classifier) and that the model may indeed shift towards a better multilingual initialization, making it suitable to quickly recover the performance lost as a result of forgetting. We then measure the recovery capabilities of the model with respect to the first language of the sequence. We empirically show that lost performance can be recovered with as little as a single training epoch even if forgetting is high (like in MultiCoNER). Performance can even greatly improve and approach the *i.i.d.* multilingual topline after only one training epoch for MultiATIS++ and 5 epochs for MultiCoNER.

In light of the above, we believe that effective continual learning methods for this task would benefit from leveraging recovery capabilities (either for a single language or many languages jointly) to limit the effect of forgetting, while preserving or even boosting forward transfer.

9 Conclusion

In this paper, we presented an analysis of cross-lingual transfer in continual learning for the sequence labeling task using multilingual BERT (Devlin et al., 2019) as well as the MultiATIS++ (Xu et al., 2020) and MultiCoNER (Malmasi et al., 2022a) corpora.

Our main finding suggests that although forgetting is present, cross-lingual transfer is retained in the form of forward transfer, which allows the model to have substantial recovery capabilities. Moreover, we empirically show that: 1) high forward transfer is linked to a progressive shift of model parameters towards a better multilingual initialization, and 2) that most knowledge from past languages is stored in the word representation encoder (BERT) and not in the task-specific classifier. Finally, we also find that current continual learning metrics may need to be adapted if we want to better estimate the distribution of transfer across the adaptation axis.

As future work, we would like to reduce training costs by leveraging fast recovery for continual learning across languages. Another interesting research direction would be a study on the continual acquisition of languages not already present in multilingual BERT.

Reproducible Research

In the spirit of reproducible research, we release our code as open source available at `github.com/juanmc2005/ContinualNLU`.

Acknowledgements

This work has been partially funded by the LIHLITH project (ANR-17-CHR2-0001-03), and supported by ERA-Net CHIST-ERA, and the "Agence Nationale pour la Recherche" (ANR, France). It has also been partially funded by French ANRT under CIFRE PhD contract # 2019/0628. It was also possible thanks to the Saclay-IA computing platform and was performed using HPC resources from GENCI-IDRIS (Grant 2022-AD011012609R1).

References

Hervé Abdi. 2007. The Kendall rank correlation coefficient. *Encyclopedia of Measurement and Statistics. Sage, Thousand Oaks, CA*, pages 508–510.

Mikhail Arkhipov, Maria Trofimova, Yurii Kuratov, and Alexey Sorokin. 2019. Tuning multilingual transformers for language-specific named entity recognition. In *Proceedings of the 7th Workshop on Balto-Slavic Natural Language Processing*, pages 89–93.

Gaurav Arora, Afshin Rahimi, and Timothy Baldwin. 2019. Does an LSTM forget more than a CNN? an empirical study of catastrophic forgetting in NLP. In *Proceedings of the The 17th Annual Workshop of the Australasian Language Technology Association*, pages 77–86, Sydney, Australia. Australasian Language Technology Association.

Tom Brown, Benjamin Mann, Nick Ryder, Melanie Subbiah, Jared D Kaplan, Prafulla Dhariwal, Arvind Neelakantan, Pranav Shyam, Girish Sastry, Amanda Askell, et al. 2020. Language models are few-shot learners. *Advances in neural information processing systems*, 33:1877–1901.

Alexis Conneau, Kartikay Khandelwal, Naman Goyal, Vishrav Chaudhary, Guillaume Wenzek, Francisco Guzmán, Edouard Grave, Myle Ott, Luke Zettlemoyer, and Veselin Stoyanov. 2020. Unsupervised cross-lingual representation learning at scale. In *ACL*.

Jacob Devlin, Ming-Wei Chang, Kenton Lee, and Kristina Toutanova. 2019. BERT: Pre-training of Deep Bidirectional Transformers for Language Understanding. In *Proceedings of the 2019 Conference of the North American Chapter of the Association for Computational Linguistics: Human Language Technologies, Volume 1 (Long and Short Papers)*, pages 4171–4186, Minneapolis, Minnesota. Association for Computational Linguistics.

Quynh Do, Judith Gaspers, Tobias Roeding, and Melanie Bradford. 2020. To what degree can language borders be blurred in BERT-based multilingual spoken language understanding? In *Proceedings of the 28th International Conference on Computational Linguistics*, pages 2699–2709, Barcelona, Spain (Online). International Committee on Computational Linguistics.

Jack FitzGerald, Christopher Hench, Charith Peris, Scott Mackie, Kay Rottmann, Ana Sanchez, Aaron Nash, Liam Urbach, Vishesh Kakarala, Richa Singh, Swetha Ranganath, Laurie Crist, Misha Britan, Wouter Leeuwis, Gokhan Tur, and Prem Natarajan. 2022. Massive: A 1m-example multilingual natural language understanding dataset with 51 typologically-diverse languages.

Robert M. French. 1999. Catastrophic forgetting in connectionist networks. *Trends in Cognitive Sciences*, 3(4):128 – 135.

Raia Hadsell, Dushyant Rao, Andrei A. Rusu, and Razvan Pascanu. 2020. Embracing Change: Continual Learning in Deep Neural Networks. *Trends in Cognitive Sciences*, 24:1028–1040.

Charles T. Hemphill, John J. Godfrey, and George R. Doddington. 1990. The ATIS spoken language systems pilot corpus. In *Speech and Natural Language: Proceedings of a Workshop Held at Hidden Valley, Pennsylvania, June 24-27,1990*.

Karthikeyan K, Zihan Wang, Stephen Mayhew, and Dan Roth. 2020. Cross-Lingual Ability of Multilingual BERT: An Empirical Study. In *International Conference on Learning Representations*.

Diederik P Kingma and Jimmy Ba. 2015. Adam: A method for stochastic optimization. In *International-Conference on Learning Representations (ICLR)*.

Sungjin Lee. 2017. Toward continual learning for conversational agents. *arXiv preprint arXiv:1712.09943*.

Zihan Liu, Genta Indra Winata, Andrea Madotto, and Pascale Fung. 2021. Preserving Cross-Linguality of Pre-trained Models via Continual Learning. In *Proceedings of the 6th Workshop on Representation Learning for NLP (RepL4NLP-2021)*, pages 64–71, Online. Association for Computational Linguistics.

David Lopez-Paz and Marc' Aurelio Ranzato. 2017. Gradient Episodic Memory for Continual Learning. In *Advances in Neural Information Processing Systems*, volume 30. Curran Associates, Inc.

Andrea Madotto, Zhaojiang Lin, Zhenpeng Zhou, Seungwhan Moon, Paul Crook, Bing Liu, Zhou Yu, Eunjoon Cho, and Zhiguang Wang. 2020. Continual learning in task-oriented dialogue systems. *arXiv preprint arXiv:2012.15504*.

Shervin Malmasi, Anjie Fang, Besnik Fetahu, Sudipta Kar, and Oleg Rokhlenko. 2022a. MultiCoNER: a Large-scale Multilingual dataset for Complex Named Entity Recognition.

Shervin Malmasi, Anjie Fang, Besnik Fetahu, Sudipta Kar, and Oleg Rokhlenko. 2022b. SemEval-2022 Task 11: Multilingual Complex Named Entity Recognition (MultiCoNER). In *Proceedings of the 16th International Workshop on Semantic Evaluation (SemEval-2022)*. Association for Computational Linguistics.

Natawut Monaikul, Giuseppe Castellucci, Simone Filice, and Oleg Rokhlenko. 2021. Continual learning for named entity recognition. In *AAAI*.

David Mueller, Nicholas Andrews, and Mark Dredze. 2020. Sources of transfer in multilingual named entity recognition. In *Proceedings of the 58th Annual Meeting of the Association for Computational Linguistics*, pages 8093–8104, Online. Association for Computational Linguistics.

Vinod Nair and Geoffrey E Hinton. 2010. Rectified Linear Units Improve Restricted Boltzmann Machines. In *ICML*.

Hiroki Nakayama. 2018. seqeval: A python framework for sequence labeling evaluation. Software available from https://github.com/chakki-works/seqeval.

Joakim Nivre, Marie-Catherine de Marneffe, Filip Ginter, Jan Hajič, Christopher D. Manning, Sampo Pyysalo, Sebastian Schuster, Francis Tyers, and Daniel Zeman. 2020. Universal Dependencies v2: An evergrowing multilingual treebank collection. In *Proceedings of the 12th Language Resources and Evaluation Conference*, pages 4034–4043, Marseille, France. European Language Resources Association.

Colin Raffel, Noam Shazeer, Adam Roberts, Katherine Lee, Sharan Narang, Michael Matena, Yanqi Zhou, Wei Li, and Peter J. Liu. 2020. Exploring the limits of transfer learning with a unified text-to-text transformer. *Journal of Machine Learning Research*, 21(140):1–67.

Lance Ramshaw and Mitch Marcus. 1995. Text Chunking using Transformation-Based Learning. In *Third Workshop on Very Large Corpora*.

Anthony Robins. 1995. Catastrophic Forgetting, Rehearsal and Pseudorehearsal. *Connection Science*, 7(2):123–146.

Sebastian Schuster, Sonal Gupta, Rushin Shah, and Mike Lewis. 2019. Cross-lingual transfer learning for multilingual task oriented dialog. In *Proceedings of the 2019 Conference of the North American Chapter of the Association for Computational Linguistics: Human Language Technologies, Volume 1 (Long and Short Papers)*, pages 3795–3805, Minneapolis, Minnesota. Association for Computational Linguistics.

Erik F. Tjong Kim Sang and Sabine Buchholz. 2000. Introduction to the CoNLL-2000 Shared Task Chunking. In *Fourth Conference on Computational Natural Language Learning and the Second Learning Language in Logic Workshop*.

Shyam Upadhyay, Manaal Faruqui, Gokhan Tür, Hakkani-Tür Dilek, and Larry Heck. 2018. (almost) zero-shot cross-lingual spoken language understanding. In *2018 IEEE International Conference on Acoustics, Speech and Signal Processing (ICASSP)*, pages 6034–6038.

Ashish Vaswani, Noam Shazeer, Niki Parmar, Jakob Uszkoreit, Llion Jones, Aidan N Gomez, Ł ukasz Kaiser, and Illia Polosukhin. 2017. Attention is All you Need. In *Advances in Neural Information Processing Systems*, volume 30. Curran Associates, Inc.

Zihan Wang, Karthikeyan K, Stephen Mayhew, and Dan Roth. 2020. Extending multilingual BERT to low-resource languages. In *Findings of the Association for Computational Linguistics: EMNLP 2020*, pages 2649–2656, Online. Association for Computational Linguistics.

Yu Xia, Quan Wang, Yajuan Lyu, Yong Zhu, Wenhao Wu, Sujian Li, and Dai Dai. 2022. Learn and review: Enhancing continual named entity recognition via reviewing synthetic samples. In *Findings of the Association for Computational Linguistics: ACL 2022*, pages 2291–2300, Dublin, Ireland. Association for Computational Linguistics.

Weijia Xu, Batool Haider, and Saab Mansour. 2020. End-to-end slot alignment and recognition for cross-lingual NLU. In *Proceedings of the 2020 Conference on Empirical Methods in Natural Language Processing (EMNLP)*, pages 5052–5063, Online. Association for Computational Linguistics.

Linting Xue, Noah Constant, Adam Roberts, Mihir Kale, Rami Al-Rfou, Aditya Siddhant, Aditya Barua, and Colin Raffel. 2020. mt5: A massively multilingual pre-trained text-to-text transformer. *arXiv preprint arXiv:2010.11934*.

Pixel-Level BPE for Auto-Regressive Image Generation

Anton Razzhigaev
Skoltech, AIRI

Anton Voronov
AIRI

Andrey Kaznacheev
MTS AI

Andrey Kusnetsov
AIRI

Denis Dimitrov
AIRI

Alexander Panchenko
Skoltech

Abstract

Pixel-level autoregression with Transformer models (Image GPT or iGPT) is one of the recent approaches to image generation that has not received massive attention and elaboration due to quadratic complexity of attention as it imposes huge memory requirements and thus restricts the resolution of the generated images. In this paper, we propose to tackle this problem by adopting Byte-Pair-Encoding (BPE) originally proposed for text processing to the image domain to drastically reduce the length of the modeled sequence. The obtained results demonstrate that it is possible to decrease the amount of computation required to generate images pixel-by-pixel while preserving their quality and the expressiveness of the features extracted from the model. Our results show that there is room for improvement for iGPT-like models with more thorough research on the way to the optimal sequence encoding techniques for images.

1 Introduction

Modern deep learning includes a broad scope of problems with varying difficulty. To solve these tasks a paradigm of pre-training is widely used in some domains, to the greatest extent in computer vision (CV) and natural language processing (NLP). Whilst unsupervised or self-supervised pre-training is more dominant in the NLP domain, CV models are mainly trained using large amounts of labeled data. Authors of iGPT (Chen et al., 2020) have attempted to prove that given appropriate conditions (namely flexible architecture and significant amount of computation) it is possible to pre-train a model that will reach state-of-the-art performance on several CV downstream tasks even with unlabeled data. They have achieved it using an autoregressive pixel-level image generation as an unsupervised training objective for training a Transformer (Vaswani et al., 2017) model.

The approach of pixel-by-pixel generation exploited in the iGPT paper simply models an image as a continuous sequence of pixels and models the probability distribution of the next pixel conditioned on all previous ones. Flattening images results in sequences of an enormous length, for example, such representation of a 128x128 RGB image will require 49152 tokens, which is infeasible for RNNs as well as for Transformer models where complexity is quadratic with respect to the sequence length.

Despite there being numerous ways of optimizing attention operation in Transformer authors of the iGPT model have deliberately chosen dense attention due to it being domain agnostic and not imposing any additional biases on the data. In our work, we continue research in this direction concentrating on the optimization of the image-to-sequence representation mechanism rather than the attention mechanism or the Transformer architecture itself.

In the presented paper we try to adopt a tokenization approach widely used in the NLP domain: Byte-Pair Encoding (BPE) to the image domain to mitigate the main issue of the original iGPT paper. These methods allow to significantly squeeze input sequences thus reducing the amount of computation required for training and inference. Following the methodology of the original paper, we also test the ability of the Transformer model pre-trained on image generation to be used as a feature extractor that competitively performs on downstream tasks, namely, image classification on CIFAR datasets [1].

The main contributions of this paper are as follows:

- We propose a novel method of image-to-sequence tokenization that allows pre-train image models on a generative objective with lower computational complexity.

[1]The code is available at https://github.com/razzant/bpe-iGPT

Proceedings of the 29th International Conference on Computational Linguistics, pages 26–30
October 12–17, 2022.

- We study the dependence between the size of BPE vocabulary and the amount of computation required for a forward pass.
- We show that pre-training with image-BPE increases the capacity of the model allowing it to learn more meaningful representations.
- We conduct several experiments measuring the model's performance on downstream tasks.

2 Related Work

Autoregressive approaches have proven to be very efficient in the NLP domain both in a pre-training and a variety of natural-language generation tasks (Radford et al. (2019), Raffel et al. (2020)). However, in the CV domain, it has been quite a challenge due to the high dimensionality of the data. One of the effective ways to tractably model a joint distribution of pixels in an image is to cast it as a product of conditional distributions. It was adopted in several models such as fully visible sigmoid belief networks (Neal, 1992) or NADE (Larochelle and Murray, 2011).

Recurrent Neural Networks (RNN) are powerful models that offer a compact, shared parametrization of a series of conditional distributions. Authors of PixelRNN (van den Oord et al., 2016) have applied this architecture to an image domain. The authors suggested two types of convolutional LSTM layers to compute all the states along one of the spatial dimensions (rows or diagonals of the image). Moreover, instead of LSTM blocks a convolutional layer with a mask to avoid seeing the future context was used. This method was called PixelCNN and got further development such as PixelCNN++ (Salimans et al., 2017). A small receptive field was an obvious disadvantage of these approaches that was overcome with the emergence of Transformers.

Transformer-based (Vaswani et al., 2017) models are extremely successful in natural language generation and understanding fields. GPT-2 (Radford et al., 2019) demonstrated human-level performance in text generating and zero-shot tasks via prompt engineering. There were numerous attempts to use GPT architecture for image generation, which can be divided into two groups: discrete feature-based regression (e.g. DALLE Ramesh et al. (2022)) or pixel-level regression (iGPT Chen et al. (2020)). The latter type of model is not fairly popular, as processing the 1D-sequence of flattened RGB-image pixels is too memory-expensive due to the length of the context and attention mechanism. To deal with this problem authors resize images to a low resolution (like $32^2 \times 3$, $48^2 \times 3$, $96^2 \times 3$ or $192^2 \times 3$) with further clustering (R, G, B) pixel values using k-means with $k = 512$ obtaining the resulting context length 32^2 or 48^2. However, the iGPT model demonstrated decent results in low-resolution image generation and downstream tasks over contextualized features. To measure model performance linear probe method was used. The method consists of training multi-class logistic regression on embeddings from a model with frozen weights on an image classification task. During pre-training on ImageNet authors also used VQVAE as a downsampler instead of RGB-clustering to keep the context of 48^2 length.

On the other side, there are numerous methods for sequence length compression in the NLP domain — different tokenization techniques, which exploit the pre-computed merge dictionaries for optimal encoding of words or byte groups. One of the most efficient methods is Byte-Pair-Encoding (Shibata et al., 1999). The idea of this algorithm is to find the most frequent pair of consecutive two-character codes in the text and then substitute an unused code for the occurrences of the pair. This method has become a good trade-off between vocabulary size and the length of the sequence fed to the model. In GPT models special modification of this algorithm is used which works at byte-level (Wang et al., 2020) — this is one more step towards optimal sequence squeezing.

3 iGPT with BPE Image Tokenization

Our BPE-enabled iGPT model relies on the GPT-2 model originally designed for text processing. More specifically we use embedding size $d = 1024$, number of layers $L = 36$ and number of heads in the multi-head attention $m = 8$ resulting in 484 million trainable parameters throughout all experiments. Due to limited computational resources, we have not conducted experiments with the BERT pre-training objective and used only linear probing as an evaluation approach.

In our experiments, we provide results for prompted image generation and linear probe on CIFAR10 and CIFAR100 datasets with pre-training on ImageNet (Deng et al., 2009) dataset. Also we demonstrate unconditional image generation on CelebA dataset (Liu et al., 2015) aligned with

MTCNN framework (Zhang et al., 2016).

3.1 Converting Images to Texts

To train byte-level BPE tokenizer we convert images to text format by assigning each pixel value a corresponding char symbol separating each row of the original image with \n symbol in the resulting text file. Since every pixel has an assigned value from 0 to 255 we can quantize them into 10 discrete buckets using integer division by 26. Now since every pixel has a value from 0 to 9 for the grey-scale setting we can replace each number with the corresponding digit character. However, for RGB images we need to represent values from all three channels in one symbol, that is why we concatenate their values resulting in one number in the range from 0 to 999, and convert this number into a character using the standard *chr* function.

For example RGB pixel [150, 112, 255] will be converted to a char in the following way:

1. RGB pixel: [150, 112, 255]
2. Quantization: [150, 112, 255] // 26 = [5, 4, 9]
3. Concatenation: [5, 4, 9] $\rightarrow$ 549
4. To char: chr(549) = ȥ

3.2 Decoding Images from Tokens

Since an output of the model can have lines of various lengths we bring them to the required fixed resolution by either upsampling or downsampling. Then in the case of grey-scale images, each character is directly translated to the corresponding quantized pixel value while for the RGB scenario we use the python *ord* function, inverse to the *chr* method used during encoding.

3.3 Encoding Efficiency

To evaluate the sequence squeezing effect of BPE for images we calculate the squeezing factor — an average ratio of the pixel-sequence length of an image to the length of tokenized pixel sequence. It can be seen from Figure 1 that the squeezing factor grows logarithmically with the size of the BPE vocabulary.

While larger vocabularies produce shorter input sequences they also increase the number of trainable parameters and the size of modeling distribution thus hindering the generation. Figure 2 shows that the vocabulary size of 30 000 tokens gives an optimal trade-off between the input squeezing

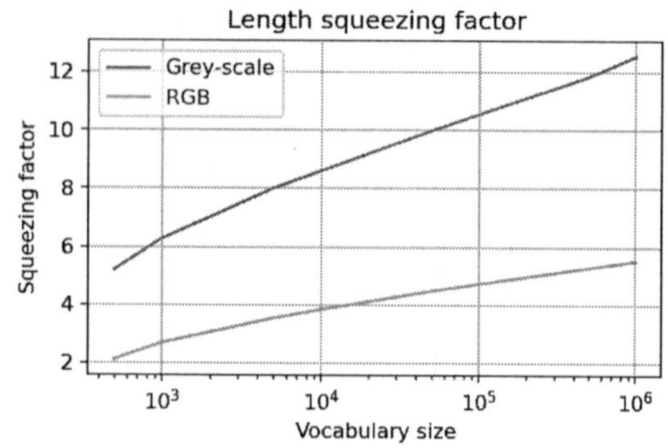

Figure 1: **Compression ratio.** The dependency of sequence squeezing factor from BPE vocabulary size for RGB and grey-scale 112x112 images. The more tokens contains BPE dictionary the shorter the sequences used to represent an image.

and computational efficiency of the model. The selected vocabulary allows us to reduce the length of pixel sequences roughly by 9 times for grey-scale images and by 4 times for RGB images, i.e. the 112x112 image can be represented by a sequence of approximately a thousand tokens.

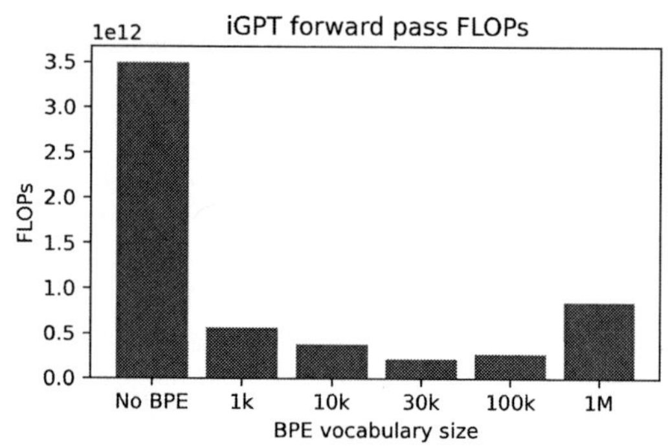

Figure 2: **Computational efficiency evaluation.** iGPT forward pass FLOPs for a 64x64 RGB image with different tokenization strategies: BPE and original pixel-level (No BPE).

4 Experiments

4.1 Examples of Generated Images

Faces generated by our BPE-iGPT model in 112x112 resolution are presented in the Figure 3 . It is worth noting that the authors of the original iGPT provided only examples generated by their largest model iGPT-XL (6.4 billion parameters) in 32x32 resolution, however visual fidelity of our samples remains on the same level. This supports our statement that image-BPE tokenization allows for pre-train Transformer models on the data of higher dimensionality with less computational overhead.

Figure 3: RGB generated faces 112 × 112.

We have also tested the ability of our model to image-conditional generation. We show examples of image completion in Figure 4. Even though we have not used any advanced sampling techniques such as nucleus sampling, tuning for the temperature, or beam-search all of the generated images contain clearly recognizable objects.

Figure 4: Image completions (64 × 64). Top row: prompt fed to model, middle: the result of the generation, bottom: ground truth image.

4.2 Image Representations for Downstream Tasks

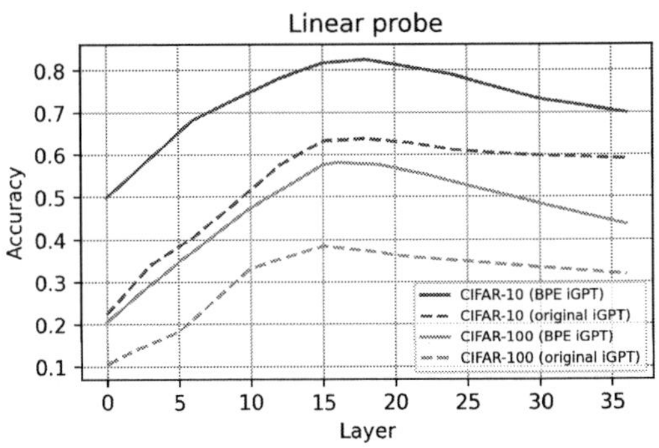

Figure 5: **Effectiveness evaluation.** Linear probe evaluation on CIFAR-10 for features extracted from every layer.

One of the common means to evaluate the representations learned by pre-trained models is linear probing on downstream tasks. To do so we train a logistic regression model over the features extracted from the trained network and compare the classification accuracy of the model pre-trained using image BPE against raw pixel sequences. Following the approach presented in the iGPT paper, we evaluate features extracted from every layer of the network.

Figure 5 shows the results of classification on CIFAR-10 and CIFAR-100 datasets. As can be seen from the plot our findings are in the agreement with the original paper: the best layers to be used as feature extractors are situated around the central layer. Another interesting finding is that even the first layer of the model trained on BPE-image contains representative features in contrast to the model trained on pixel sequence where first results better than random are obtained after several layers. One of the possible explanations for this is that some BPE-tokens represent the most common sequences of pixels which means that they already contain some semantic information in contrast to raw pixel sequences.

Our finding is in the accordance with similar research in the NLP domain. Authors of (Kharitonov et al., 2021) show that the ability of Transformer models to memorize training data is highly dependent on the size of BPE vocabulary. In combination with our results, this suggests that BPE tokenization increases the capacity of models allowing them to learn more information about the data from every layer.

5 Conclusion

In this paper, we explored the use of the BPE technique originally proposed for textual data in the image domain. It allows significantly squeeze the tokenized image sequence length mitigating the limitations of the original iGPT model. We quantitatively show that this method reduces the amount of required computation by an order of magnitude and qualitatively verify that it does not affect the quality of generated images. Moreover, applying BPE tokenization improves the representative ability of the models trained on unlabeled data. Our results suggest that the potential of image-to-sequence squeezing is not fully unleashed yet and that there is room for improvement of iGPT-like models.

References

Mark Chen, Alec Radford, Rewon Child, Jeffrey Wu, Heewoo Jun, David Luan, and Ilya Sutskever. 2020. Generative pretraining from pixels. In *Proceedings of the 37th International Conference on Machine Learning, ICML 2020, 13-18 July 2020, Virtual Event*, volume 119 of *Proceedings of Machine Learning Research*, pages 1691–1703. PMLR.

Jia Deng, Wei Dong, Richard Socher, Li-Jia Li, Kai Li, and Li Fei-Fei. 2009. Imagenet: A large-scale hierarchical image database. In *2009 IEEE Computer Society Conference on Computer Vision and Pattern Recognition (CVPR 2009), 20-25 June 2009, Miami, Florida, USA*, pages 248–255. IEEE Computer Society.

Eugene Kharitonov, Marco Baroni, and Dieuwke Hupkes. 2021. How BPE affects memorization in transformers. *CoRR*, abs/2110.02782.

Hugo Larochelle and Iain Murray. 2011. The neural autoregressive distribution estimator. In *Proceedings of the Fourteenth International Conference on Artificial Intelligence and Statistics, AISTATS 2011, Fort Lauderdale, USA, April 11-13, 2011*, volume 15 of *JMLR Proceedings*, pages 29–37. JMLR.org.

Ziwei Liu, Ping Luo, Xiaogang Wang, and Xiaoou Tang. 2015. Deep learning face attributes in the wild. In *2015 IEEE International Conference on Computer Vision, ICCV 2015, Santiago, Chile, December 7-13, 2015*, pages 3730–3738. IEEE Computer Society.

Radford M. Neal. 1992. Connectionist learning of belief networks. *Artif. Intell.*, 56(1):71–113.

Alec Radford, Jeff Wu, Rewon Child, David Luan, Dario Amodei, and Ilya Sutskever. 2019. Language models are unsupervised multitask learners.

Colin Raffel, Noam Shazeer, Adam Roberts, Katherine Lee, Sharan Narang, Michael Matena, Yanqi Zhou, Wei Li, and Peter J. Liu. 2020. Exploring the limits of transfer learning with a unified text-to-text transformer. *J. Mach. Learn. Res.*, 21:140:1–140:67.

Aditya Ramesh, Prafulla Dhariwal, Alex Nichol, Casey Chu, and Mark Chen. 2022. Hierarchical text-conditional image generation with CLIP latents. *CoRR*, abs/2204.06125.

Tim Salimans, Andrej Karpathy, Xi Chen, and Diederik P. Kingma. 2017. Pixelcnn++: Improving the pixelcnn with discretized logistic mixture likelihood and other modifications. In *5th International Conference on Learning Representations, ICLR 2017, Toulon, France, April 24-26, 2017, Conference Track Proceedings*. OpenReview.net.

Yusuke Shibata, Takuya Kida, Shuichi Fukamachi, Masayuki Takeda, Ayumi Shinohara, and Takeshi Shinohara. 1999. Byte pair encoding: A text compression scheme that accelerates pattern matching.

Aäron van den Oord, Nal Kalchbrenner, and Koray Kavukcuoglu. 2016. Pixel recurrent neural networks. In *Proceedings of the 33nd International Conference on Machine Learning, ICML 2016, New York City, NY, USA, June 19-24, 2016*, volume 48 of *JMLR Workshop and Conference Proceedings*, pages 1747–1756. JMLR.org.

Ashish Vaswani, Noam Shazeer, Niki Parmar, Jakob Uszkoreit, Llion Jones, Aidan N. Gomez, Lukasz Kaiser, and Illia Polosukhin. 2017. Attention is all you need. In *Advances in Neural Information Processing Systems 30: Annual Conference on Neural Information Processing Systems 2017, December 4-9, 2017, Long Beach, CA, USA*, pages 5998–6008.

Changhan Wang, Kyunghyun Cho, and Jiatao Gu. 2020. Neural machine translation with byte-level subwords. In *The Thirty-Fourth AAAI Conference on Artificial Intelligence, AAAI 2020, The Thirty-Second Innovative Applications of Artificial Intelligence Conference, IAAI 2020, The Tenth AAAI Symposium on Educational Advances in Artificial Intelligence, EAAI 2020, New York, NY, USA, February 7-12, 2020*, pages 9154–9160. AAAI Press.

Kaipeng Zhang, Zhanpeng Zhang, Zhifeng Li, and Yu Qiao. 2016. Joint face detection and alignment using multitask cascaded convolutional networks. *IEEE Signal Process. Lett.*, 23(10):1499–1503.

Cost-Effective Language Driven Image Editing with LX-DRIM

Rodrigo Santos and **António Branco** and **João Silva**
University of Lisbon, Faculty of Sciences
NLX—Natural Language and Speech Group
Departamento de Informática, Faculdade de Ciências de Lisboa
Campo Grande, 1749-016 Lisboa, Portugal

Abstract

Cross-modal language and image processing is envisaged as a way to improve language understanding by resorting to visual grounding, but only recently, with the emergence of neural architectures specifically tailored to cope with both modalities, has it attracted increased attention and obtained promising results.

In this paper we address a cross-modal task of language-driven image design, in particular the task of altering a given image on the basis of language instructions. We also avoid the need for a specifically tailored architecture and resort instead to a general purpose model in the Transformer family.

Experiments with the resulting tool, LX-DRIM, show very encouraging results, confirming the viability of the approach for language-driven image design while keeping it affordable in terms of compute and data.

1 Introduction

The fields of image and language processing have mostly progressed independently of one other, each focusing on its own modality. Recently, though, there have been promising prospects for advancement in cross-modal processing. A major motivation for this has been the realization that the so-called grounding is necessary for progress in language understanding (Bisk et al., 2020), and a major enabling factor has been the emergence of underlying technology that can be successfully applied to both modalities and their cross-modal processing (Dosovitskiy et al., 2020; Ramesh et al., 2021; Wu et al., 2021; Radford et al., 2021).

In the image to language direction, there has been considerable progress in the task of image captioning, that is of generating a language description for an input image (Radford et al., 2021; Xu et al., 2015; Wu et al., 2017; Hossain et al., 2019), and the subsidiary task of image retrieval from a language description (Reed et al., 2016; Guo et al., 2018; Yu and Grauman, 2017; Kovashka et al., 2012); while in the language to image direction promising results have been obtained on the task of image generation from an input language description (Ramesh et al., 2021; Wu et al., 2021).

Conditional Generative models based on the Transformer architecture (Vaswani et al., 2017) became one of the mainstream approaches for virtually any language processing task (Radford et al., 2019; Brown et al., 2020; Devlin et al., 2018) due to their ability to cope with the intrinsically compositional nature of language and the meaning conveyed by contextualized expressions. Recently, these models have also shown promise for image processing tasks, namely in image generation (Ramesh et al., 2021; Wu et al., 2021), showcasing their capacity to handle multi-modal input, and how general purpose the Transformer architecture can be, coping also with data rooted in signals that are not linguistic in nature.

The DALL-E model (Ramesh et al., 2021) delivered promising results in such a task, by receiving a description in the form of a snippet of text (e.g. "a green clock in the form of an hexagon") and creating an image that humans recognize as one that could correspond to that input description. And its extension DALL-E 2 (Ramesh et al., 2022) undertakes also a more restricted task, where a specified subarea of the image is to be completed on the basis of the language description. These models achieve these results by leveraging massive quantities of data and compute that are hardly accessible to most research groups and organizations.

Adopting a distinct line of inquiry, in the present paper we aim at addressing a challenge of language driven image design, consisting of editing an image on the basis of language instructions to do so. Here the output image is conditioned not only on a text snippet but also on an input image, such that that image is appropriately altered taking into account the language input.

Proceedings of the 29th International Conference on Computational Linguistics, pages 31–43
October 12–17, 2022.

Figure 1: First (left to right): image with the caption "dark red pumps". Second: image generated (CIG model) with only the textual description in the caption of the first image. Third: outcome of the alteration of the second image (CIA model) with the instruction "are a darker red". Fourth: image retrieved from the database by using the second image for matching.

For example, given an image of a piece of furniture, the model is asked to change its color. And then possibly its height, shape, viewing perspective, or the direction of the light. This process should allow one to iteratively and interactively modify the design of some object without any specific image manipulation software, and with no knowledge of how to work with it.

This workflow can be exploited in a wide range of innovative applications, such as supporting a shopping assistant that progressively matches images altered by language instructions against current stock and suggests increasingly suitable products, among others examples.

Also concerned with addressing the issue of resource cost, in this paper we present exploratory research results on affordable Language Driven Image Design (LDID). The major contributions and findings of this study are: (i) a suitably instantiated GPT-2 (Radford et al., 2019) is an effective option to perform LDID; (ii) in what concerns the task of Conditional Image Generation, our approach offers a more streamlined setup than the one adopted in DALL-E; (iii) as a by-product of its ability for LDID, our model may usefully support the subsidiary task of image retrieval; and (iv) extending this set up with a pre-trained language model may improve the performance in some LDID tasks. This study resulted on the creation of a tool, LX-DRIM, for editing an image on the basis of language instructions.

The remainder of this document is structured as follows: Section 2 describes the neural model used in this study; Section 3 explains the experiments performed and introduces the data sets used; Section 4 presents the results obtained; Section 5 proceeds with error analysis; Section 6 discusses related work; and Section 7 closes the paper with concluding remarks.

2 Model

In looking for affordable LDID, we resorted to a GPT-2 small model (Radford et al., 2019), namely its current implementation from the transformers package of HuggingFace,[1] including their English pre-trained GPT-2 as well.[2]

GPT-2 has been successfully applied to virtually all language processing tasks. Given it was conceived for text, some adaptation is required in order for it to handle images. Interestingly, changes to the model architecture can be dispensed with, and the required adaptations can be restricted solely to the way the input data is pre-processed.

The minimal twist is to pass the images through a Vector-Quantized Variation Auto Encoder (VQ-VAE) that is both capable of describing an image with tokens according to an internal vocabulary of images and of constructing an image from those tokens (Ramesh et al., 2021).

Similarly to Variational Autoencoders, the main goal of VQ-VAEs is the encoding of an image into a vector, or group of vectors, that can then be decoded as closely as possible into the same original image. However, while in standard Variational Autoencoders, the latent space is continuous and is sampled from a Gaussian distribution, VQ-VAEs operate on a discrete latent space by maintaining a codebook. This codebook can then be used as vocabulary for text conditioned image generation.

Therefore, by passing an image through a VQ-VAE, one gets a sequence of tokens that represents the image. This sequence can be fed to a GPT-2 model like it is done with the sequence of tokens for language, given that the image tokens also have their own embedding in the embedding layer.

In this work we use the VQ-VAE from (Esser et al., 2021)[3], with a "vocabulary" for images of size 1024, which is added to the GPT-2 embedding map, and by means of which every image is represented.

With this extension to images in place, one can now proceed to train GPT-2 as it is done when it is applied solely to text, whereby given an input token it learns to predict the next one.

As training parameters for the GPT-2, we use a batch size of 6 with gradient accumulation of 16, meaning that at each step our model back-propagates with 96 training instances. We evaluate

[1]https://huggingface.co/docs/transformers/index
[2]https://huggingface.co/gpt2
[3]https://github.com/CompVis/taming-transformers

on the development set every 250 steps, and stop training when the development set loss does not decrease from its lowest point after 5 evaluations.

After the training of the GPT-2 model, we optionally rank its outputs using CLIP[4] over the various images from the same input. After using two separate encoders, for image and for text, CLIP maps their encoding vectors into a common embedding so that a caption and its respective image end up with the same representation (Radford et al., 2021). CLIP can thus support the ranking of images generated from a caption given the encoded image that is closer (in vector space) to the encoded caption is the one more closely described by the caption.

3 Experiments

With this model in place, the following experiments were undertaken:[5] (i) a warm up experience, aimed at assessing the capability of the model for Conditional Image Generation (CIG)—generating an image from a text snippet describing it; (ii) the central experiment of interest here, aimed at assessing how well the model is able to perform Conditional Image Alteration (CIA)—generating an image both from another image and from a text snippet describing how the later should be altered; and, in addition, (iii) a comparison between the model and a variant obtained by extending it with a language pre-training phase.

3.1 Data sets

We resorted to the two data sets developed by (Guo et al., 2018)[6] for their research on image retrieval, which we re-purposed for the tasks of interest here, which differ from that original image retrieval task.

These data were developed through crowdsourcing with Amazon Turk and include: (i) a dataset of images of women shoes and respective captions, re-purposed here for the CIG task; and (ii) a dataset where each instance contains a source image of a shoe, a target image of another shoe, and a short textual description of how the source image relates to the target one, re-purposed here for the CIA task. Figure 2 shows an example from each data set.

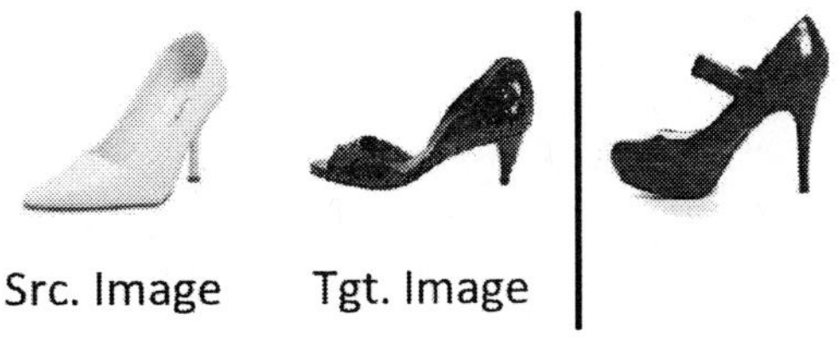

Figure 2: Left image: example in the CIA dataset, where the pair of images are associated to this textual instruction for the source image to be altered into the target image: "are black with a thicker heel". Right image: example in the CIG dataset, associated to the caption "dark red platform high heels with a strap".

The data set for CIG has 3600 examples. We randomly shuffled it and produced a 80/10/10 split, taking 2880 examples for training, 360 for development and the remaining 360 for testing. The data set for CIA, in turn, has 10750 examples, and it was also shuffled and submitted to a 80/10/10 split, with a 8600 example set for training, 1075 for development and 1075 for testing.

All images in these data sets are augmented via several transformations: (i) images are flipped horizontally with a 50% chance; (ii) rotated between 0° and 20° clockwise or anticlockwise; (iii) distorted in order to simulate different perspectives with a 50% chance; (iv) their sharpness increased by a factor of 2 with a 50% chance; and finally (v) their contrast is maximized with a 50% chance.

3.2 Input representation

3.2.1 Conditional Image Generation

For each instance in the CIG data set, 194 input tokens were used: 128 text tokens, with the image caption; followed by a delimiter token (<I>) indicating where the image begins; followed by the 64 tokens output by the VAE, which represent the image; and finally, another <I> token indicating the end of the image.

During preliminary experimentation, we varied the number of tokens that represent the image and observed that using more tokens created a higher resolution image at the cost of the image being less precise. We empirically found that using 64 tokens to represent the image led to a good tradeoff between image quality and precision.

Also in preliminary experimentation, while experimenting with other data sets not used in this study, another finding was that using images with white backgrounds helped the model to focus on the main object, being difficult for the model to precisely detect the object in question when the image had a noisier background.

[4]https://github.com/openai/CLIP

[5]Materials for the reproduction of the results reported here are available at https://github.com/nlx-group/LX-DRIM.

[6]https://github.com/XiaoxiaoGuo/fashion-retrieval

3.2.2 Conditional Image Alteration

For each instance in the CIA data set, 259 tokens were used: 128 text tokens with the request for alteration; a <I> token marking the beginning of the source image; 64 image tokens from the source image; a <I> token marking both the end of the source image and the beginning of the target image; another 64 tokens from the target image; and finally, a <I> token marking the end of the target image.

Our initial approach was to provide the source image first, followed then by the textual alteration. However, the resulting model had worse performance than the one with the text in the first (leftmost) place, as described above. This is possibly due to the fact that, by having the textual tokens first, the model can more easily learn the point from which no more textual tokens occur—after the first <I>—and after that point can attribute low probabilities to textual tokens and focus solely on generating image tokens.

3.2.3 Impact of CLIP

The notion of prompt engineering has emerged in papers like the ones regarding GPT-2 (Radford et al., 2019) or GPT-3 (Brown et al., 2020), and also DALL-E (Ramesh et al., 2021) or CLIP (Radford et al., 2021). This concerns how the textual input is given to the model and how the user can condition it to deliver the desired result.

Similarly to what is reported in those papers, the performance of our CIA model improves when the description of the object in the source image is included in the alteration text, instead of this text only stating the alteration to perform—e.g. "high heels are a darker tone" vs. "are a darker tone". This can be partly attributed to the fact that the model gets a confirmation of what image to generate ("high heels" vs. "rain boots"). We use this approach to help CLIP rank the generated images, by prefixing the textual input with the expression denoting the type of object of the source image.

While the type of object of the source image may not always be the same as that of the target image, in general a prompt prepared this way improves the performance when CLIP is used for ranking.

4 Results

The evaluation of a generative task (e.g. summarization, etc.), where typically there can be more than one output that is acceptable as correct, tends to be a problematic endeavour. While one could try to compare to a gold standard in order to perform an automatic evaluation, small differences (of equally acceptable outputs) to the gold example inevitably makes most such metrics, like accuracy, etc., useless, leaving only some kind of distance metric to be resorted to.

In contrast to text processing, this problem tends to be further aggravated for images, as metrics that are used to evaluate textual generative tasks, like BLEU (Papineni et al., 2002) or METEOR (Banerjee and Lavie, 2005), work by being able to refer to some parts that are well defined substructures in an expression (e.g. words), but for images there are no clear substructures that can be resorted to, and in most cases these distance metrics work only at the pixel level.

4.1 Distance metrics

Given these considerations, we resorted to four distance metrics, two of which are hash functions:[7] Average hash (A. Hash), which takes the shape into consideration but compares the images in gray scale; Color hash (C. Hash), similar to A. Hash but taking color into consideration; Mean Square Error (MSE), the most rudimentary metric used, which focuses on the distance between pixels; and Structural Similarity Index Measure (SSIM) (Wang et al., 2004), one of the most used metric for image comparison, which extracts luminance, contrast and structure to compare two images. For the first three, lower scores are better, while for SSIM higher scores are better.

The results obtained with these automatic metrics will help to converge onto the more favorable settings for the model whose performance will eventually be submitted to the manual evaluation.

4.2 Conditional Image Generation

Table 1 presents the results obtained for CIG, where images are generated from text descriptions.[8] All evaluation scores were obtained as the mean score of the top four ranked images, with the exception of the last line (as only one image was available). The data for this task are available at https://github.com/nlx-group/LX-DRIM, which also include the images generated.

The best results under each metric concentrate in the middle of the table, when CLIP is fed with

[7]https://pypi.org/project/ImageHash/

[8]Running on an NVIDIA 2080 RTX 8G, CIG models were trained in 7 and 3 GPU hours, with and without language pre-training respectively.

N. Examples	A. Hash	C. Hash	MSE	SSIM	A. Hash	C. Hash	MSE	SSIM
	Without textual pre-training				With textual pre-training			
32	13.553	**4.6313**	0.0868	0.5587	13.480	4.6458	0.0832	0.5658
16	**13.510**	4.6326	0.0859	0.5614	13.434	4.6340	0.0824	0.5691
8	13.594	4.6681	**0.0850**	**0.5638**	**13.326**	**4.6285**	**0.0810**	**0.5741**
4	18.826	5.0792	0.0859	0.5290	19.441	5.0451	0.0830	0.5226
1	33.575	6.0417	0.0916	0.4072	35.875	6.2944	0.0901	0.3704

Table 1: Evaluation of CIG with the averaged scores of top-4 images, with (right half) and without (left) textual pre-training, with four image distance metrics (columns): Average Hash, Color Hash, Mean Square Error (lower is better), and Structural Similarity Index Measure (higher is better). The first column indicates the number of generated images (8, 16 and 32) given to CLIP.

eight examples. This indicates that using CLIP improves performance only to a certain point, after which increasing the number of examples given to it induces a detrimental effect.

With only one image generated, the model has the worst performance as there is no ranking to exclude the worst images. However, with four images generated (which also do not pass through CLIP), there are better scores than with only one, indicating that the model is more prone to creating more precise images than imprecise ones, and that by having multiple images the error is averaged out.

Considering the best scores with each metric, the models pre-trained with language data (right half of the table) have better performance than those that do not have such pre-training (left half). This may hint at that language pre-training is still relevant when there are images also in the fine-tuning phase.

4.3 Conditional Image Alteration

Table 2 presents the results for CIA, where images are generated both from other images and from text describing the alterations requested.[9]

The scores for the contribution of CLIP here are less consistently aligned with each other. Like in CIG, in general, a lower number of examples fed into CLIP seems to lead to better results.

In fact, with the SSIM metric, the best results are obtained with CLIP being fed with the lower number (8) of examples. However, for the hash metrics, it is hard to find such clear trend, other than that CLIP supports the best scores—in many setups with less examples, but in a few others with more. And while lower number of examples fed into CLIP also leads to better results with the MSE metric, their best results, in turn, are obtained without CLIP.

Additionally, considering the best scores with each metric, in some metrics one gets better results with textual pre-training, while with others is the other way around. These results are thus inconclusive with regards whether performance improves with or without textual pre-training for CIA.

4.4 Calibration

As an opportunistic extension or application of our model, its conditional image editing capability can easily support an image retrieval system. This can be achieved by measuring the distance, from the image generated for the input description, to every image in a database and retrieve the one that is found to be the most similar.[10]

While the performance of this kind of approach is likely inferior when compared to the feature-based methodology typically used in image retrieval systems, it is still worth experimenting with it. This will have the virtue of helping to assess the reliability of each one of the four evaluation metrics we have been using: given every metric is agnostic to the dataset, the domain or the model, and with no possible bias sensitive to any of them, the one with more matches to the gold counterparts will turn out to be the best to be used to evaluate image design tasks.

We evaluate the CIG model, with language pre-training, with 8 images generated (and filtered to 4 by CLIP), for its retrieval accuracy within the top 50, 10, 5 and 1 images retrieved, resorting to

[9]Running on an NVIDIA Titan RTX 24G, CIA models were trained in 17 and 7 GPU hours, with and without language pre-training respectively. Model inference (image generation) took less than a second.

[10]It is worth noting again that the data set we are using (Guo et al., 2018) was originally developed to support a image retrieval task, which the authors addressed by means of a complex system that takes into account the user feedback so that at each turn the system tends to get closer to the correct image to be retrieved.

N. Examples	A. Hash	C. Hash	MSE	SSIM	A. Hash	C. Hash	MSE	SSIM
	Without textual pre-training				With textual pre-training			
32	14.272	**4.2679**	0.1103	0.5339	14.583	4.7551	0.1109	0.5352
16	**13.952**	4.2842	0.1076	0.5399	**14.381**	4.7409	0.1100	0.5401
8	14.431	4.6902	0.1074	**0.5464**	14.431	**4.6902**	0.1074	**0.5464**
4	17.633	4.3937	**0.1041**	0.5459	20.102	5.1612	0.1040	0.4976
1	27.836	4.8112	0.1049	0.5173	34.122	6.2688	**0.0967**	0.3650

Table 2: Evaluation of CIA.

N. Retrieved	A. Hash	C. Hash	MSE	SSIM
50	33.61%	30.28%	46.67%	9.17%
10	10.00%	11.11%	15.00%	1.94%
5	5.56%	6.39%	8.33%	1.39%
1	1.67%	1.39%	1.67%	0.28%

Table 3: Accuracy of retrieving images with images generated from their captions by the CIG model where the retrieval is based in each of the four distance metrics (columns), for top-k retrieved images (first column).

the 360 examples in the test set. The respective evaluation scores are displayed in Table 3.

These results on image retrieval are low, being, nevertheless, above the random baseline (1/360 or 0.27% for 1 image retrieved). We tend to attribute these low results mainly to the nature of the data set as most images are very similar to each other—more on this below, in Section 5.

Nonetheless, the important take away sought for is the comparison between the four metrics, and their calibration to serve as evaluation metrics for our tasks of interest. Whereas MSE is the metric with higher scores at all settings considered (i.e. each line in the table), SSIM gets the lower scores, practically at random performance, being only 0.01% above it when one image is retrieved. Hash metrics, in turn, perform practically on a par with each other, with A. Hash performing slightly above C. Hash for 1 and 50 retrieved images, and C. Hash performing above A. Hash for 5 and 10 images. Accordingly, these results indicate that MSE could be considered as a more reliable distance metric than the other three.

4.5 Evaluation

Taking these preparatory findings into account, the model was evaluated in the task of interest here, CIA, under what appears as its most suitable settings following MSE scoring, with one example generated and language pre-training.

Two test sets were gathered, each with 25 randomly selected examples. Test set A (cf. Appendix A.1) consisted of triples with, from left to right in each line, source image, image produced by the model, and the alteration instruction. In test set B (cf. Appendix A.2), the examples consisted of 4-ary tuples with, from left to right, the source image, the gold target image, the image output by our model, and the instruction for alteration.

Six independent and voluntary evaluators were assigned the following task: given the original image on the left and the alteration instruction, classify how much the image on the right is a satisfactory result with a score from $\{1, 2, 3, 4\}$, where 4 indicates that it is fully satisfactory. They ran the evaluation over the entire test set A first, and then over the test B. To avoid eventual prejudice and respective bias, they were not told that images were generated by computer.

The averaged mean ratings of the evaluators was 2.37 (s.d. 0.11) with test set A. With test set B, the perceived quality slightly lowered to 2.26 (s.d. 0.36), showing that evaluators' rating tended to be pulled down by their seeing a result deemed as fully satisfactory side by side to the one under evaluation.

To evaluate also the CIG task, as DALL-E is not available, we resorted to its HuggingFace smaller version, DALL-E mini,[11] to generate images from 25 randomly selected captions in our data set (cf. Appendix B). Our model was also run on these captions. Following the same comparative evaluation approach used for CIG in DALL-E, in a best-of-five vote, the images generated by our model were always chosen as the most realistic and as best matching the caption. The images generated by the other system happen to be scrambled pieces of disparate objects.

When compared to our model DALL-E mini has

[11] https://huggingface.co/flax-community/dalle-mini

3 times more parameters (400 million vs 124 million) and was trained on 5000 times more images (15 million vs 2880).

5 Error analysis

To help in error analysis, difficult cases are exemplified in Figure 1. The two leftmost shoes are, respectively, the target image and the (CIG) generated image with the description "dark red pumps".

Both shoes are quite similar in terms of shape, but their color is different. This is a good illustration that color saturation and lightness are subjective and hard to transmit via text. In the target image (1st column), the desired dark red is almost black, and the image generated (CIG) from "dark red pumps" (2nd column) is lighter.

Interestingly, even the tentative correction (CIA) of this image with the instruction "are a darker red" still does not produce an image (3rd column) that is not as dark as in the first column.

Though image retrieval is not a central task of interest in this paper, it is worth noting that this may be even more serious for image retrieval as slight changes in saturation and lightness can make the system choose a different image: When trying to retrieve an image from the database, using the generated image (2nd column), the image that is retrieved is the one at the fourth column.

Further difficult examples, generated by the CIA model, are shown in Figure 3.

One problem illustrated there concerns image clarity. Even though some images (see 1st column) are correct, they have some fuzzy details. This is likely due to the reduced volume of the training data set. However, as already mentioned, in order to have images with higher resolution given a data set of this size, one would have to sacrifice image relevance and precision.

Another problem arises when the target image is very different from the source image (see 2nd column). In such cases, the model is basically asked to create a quite different object, for which the small size of the data set provided limited evidence.

Additional problems occur when the images to be generated are too similar to the source image (see 3rd column), or the generated images are too similar to each other (see 3rd and 4th images in the 1st column). While not necessarily a problem for the overall quality of the output, the first kind of cases becomes an issue for evaluation, as generated images may be more similar to the source image

Figure 3: Examples of CIA for error analysis. First row: source images. Second row: target images. Remaining rows: top four generated images. Textual instructions for image alteration in left column: "athletic shoes are blue and silver"; middle column: "athletic shoes are bronze-colored slingbacks"; right column: "pumps are blue".

than to the target one. As for the second kind of cases, when the generated images are similar to one another, it may become a problem if object design is the intended use for the tool, and not just image alteration.

To address these issues, further techniques to enhance image diversity should be explored in future work, so that the model can suggest a more varied set of images to the user.

6 Related Work

A promising application of deep learning to image generation was presented in (Goodfellow et al., 2014), with a Generative Adversarial Network (GAN), a forerunner of a research line continued in (Xu et al., 2017), (Zhu et al., 2019), (Tao et al., 2021), a.o. A two part network containing a generator and a discriminator was proposed: The generator tries to create fake yet as realist as possible images, while the discriminator tries to distinguish the fake images produced by the generator from real ones.

Despite this early success being attributed also to the use of Convolution Neural Networks (CNN) (LeCun et al., 1989), the concept of GAN can be used with other deep learning approaches. Such is the case of the more recent work in (Jiang et al., 2021b), where two Transformer models (Vaswani et al., 2017) are used as a discriminator and a generator respectively. With no convolution at its core, they achieve competitive scores when compared to their CNN counterparts.

Transformers gained their notoriety with their success in languages processing tasks of all kinds, and recently they have been applied to other data modalities. Relevant models that use Transformers for Image Generation from captions are DALL-E (Ramesh et al., 2021), and NUWA (Wu et al., 2021). The major difference between them is that NUWA also uses video while DALL-E works only with pictures, and that NUWA uses a different type of attention mechanism, 3D Nearby Attention.

The approach proposed in (Galatolo et al., 2021) also achieves promising results in image generation with a pre-trained Transformer CLIP (Radford et al., 2021), only by training a genetic algorithm.

More recently DALL-E 2 (Ramesh et al., 2022) improves upon its predecessor by incorporating the CLIP model for image and caption representation, and through the use of a diffusion model for image generation (Dhariwal and Nichol, 2021).

The architecture adopted in our model is similar to the backbone architecture on which the implementation of DALL-E is based. Our model is different from DALL-E, however, in not having any specific optimization performed on the base Transformer, like it was done to set up DALL-E, and in being of a more reduced size (124M vs. 12B parameters). Our system also differs in that it is geared for a task other than the Conditional Image Generation one, of DALL-E, namely the task of Conditional Image Alteration. It happens also that it was trained in a much smaller amount of data (10750 vs. 250 million examples).

Also, related to our research topic, (Cheng et al., 2020) tackles the same task, though by means of a Generator/Discriminator architecture, with data that while similar to ours is not the same. To the best of our knowledge, that dataset is not publicly available, so no comparison was possible. (Jiang et al., 2021a) also work with language guided image edition, with different datasets that do not tackle the problem of object shape manipulation.

Work on image editing without language guidance can be found in the work of (Zhu et al., 2020; Zhuang et al., 2021), on different datasets.

The research presented here appears as a more streamlined approach for the tasks involved in Language Driven Image Design since most of the work is performed with a common decoder-only architecture, in the form of a GPT-2 small model. This is a generalist architecture that can be adapted for other tasks, as it was the case here with the CIG task, or any other task that can be represented by a sequence (text, audio, image, etc.).

7 Conclusion

The present study explored Conditional Generative models for Language Driven Image Design, by means of an affordable GPT-2 instantiation with only 124M parameters. The central task of interest here was Conditional Image Alteration, consisting of generating a new image given a source image and a textual instruction for its alteration, on which the proposed LX-DRIM application showed a performance rated at 2.37 (in 1–5) by manual evaluators.

Resorting to the same data set, the task of Conditional Image Generation, consisting of generating an image given a textual description, was also experimented with. Very encouraging results were also obtained, specially taking into account that the data set used here was several orders of magnitude smaller than the one that has been used in the literature for this task.

In addition, we found also that as by-product of its cross-modal processing ability, our model may usefully support the subsidiary task of image retrieval through the use of its generated images.

Empirical experimentation obtained very encouraging results and demonstrated that the proposed approach can support an effective solution to Language Driven Image Design and represents a promising research path whose potential is worth being further exploited.

The present study focuses on changing a single object in the image, rather than multiple objects in a scene. Future work the task of scene manipulation (El-Nouby et al., 2019; Zhang et al., 2021) should be investigated by exploiting the approach developed here with single object manipulation.

Acknowledgments

The research reported here was supported partially by PORTULAN CLARIN—Research Infrastructure for the Science and Technology of Language, funded by Lisboa 2020, Alentejo 2020 and FCT—Fundação para a Ciência e Tecnologia under the grant PINFRA/22117/2016.

References

Satanjeev Banerjee and Alon Lavie. 2005. METEOR: An automatic metric for MT evaluation with improved correlation with human judgments. In *Proceedings of the ACL workshop on intrinsic and extrinsic evaluation measures for machine translation and/or summarization*, pages 65–72.

Yonatan Bisk, Ari Holtzman, Jesse Thomason, Jacob Andreas, Yoshua Bengio, Joyce Chai, Mirella Lapata, Angeliki Lazaridou, Jonathan May, Aleksandr Nisnevich, et al. 2020. Experience grounds language. In *Proceedings of the 2020 Conference on Empirical Methods in Natural Language Processing (EMNLP)*, pages 8718–8735.

Tom B Brown, Benjamin Mann, Nick Ryder, Melanie Subbiah, Jared Kaplan, Prafulla Dhariwal, Arvind Neelakantan, Pranav Shyam, Girish Sastry, Amanda Askell, et al. 2020. Language models are few-shot learners. *arXiv preprint arXiv:2005.14165*.

Yu Cheng, Zhe Gan, Yitong Li, Jingjing Liu, and Jianfeng Gao. 2020. Sequential attention gan for interactive image editing. In *Proceedings of the 28th ACM International Conference on Multimedia*, pages 4383–4391.

Jacob Devlin, Ming-Wei Chang, Kenton Lee, and Kristina Toutanova. 2018. Bert: Pre-training of deep bidirectional transformers for language understanding. *arXiv preprint arXiv:1810.04805*.

Prafulla Dhariwal and Alexander Nichol. 2021. Diffusion models beat gans on image synthesis. *Advances in Neural Information Processing Systems*, 34.

Alexey Dosovitskiy, Lucas Beyer, Alexander Kolesnikov, Dirk Weissenborn, Xiaohua Zhai, Thomas Unterthiner, Mostafa Dehghani, Matthias Minderer, Georg Heigold, Sylvain Gelly, et al. 2020. An image is worth 16x16 words: Transformers for image recognition at scale. *arXiv preprint arXiv:2010.11929*.

Alaaeldin El-Nouby, Shikhar Sharma, Hannes Schulz, Devon Hjelm, Layla El Asri, Samira Ebrahimi Kahou, Yoshua Bengio, and Graham W Taylor. 2019. Tell, draw, and repeat: Generating and modifying images based on continual linguistic instruction. In *Proceedings of the IEEE/CVF International Conference on Computer Vision*, pages 10304–10312.

Patrick Esser, Robin Rombach, and Bjorn Ommer. 2021. Taming transformers for high-resolution image synthesis. In *Proceedings of the IEEE/CVF Conference on Computer Vision and Pattern Recognition*, pages 12873–12883.

Federico A Galatolo, Mario GCA Cimino, and Gigliola Vaglini. 2021. Generating images from caption and vice versa via CLIP-guided generative latent space search. *arXiv preprint arXiv:2102.01645*.

Ian Goodfellow, Jean Pouget-Abadie, Mehdi Mirza, Bing Xu, David Warde-Farley, Sherjil Ozair, Aaron Courville, and Yoshua Bengio. 2014. Generative adversarial nets. *Advances in neural information processing systems*, 27.

Xiaoxiao Guo, Hui Wu, Yu Cheng, Steven Rennie, Gerald Tesauro, and Rogerio Schmidt Feris. 2018. Dialog-based interactive image retrieval. In *Proceedings of the 32nd International Conference on Neural Information Processing Systems*, pages 676–686.

MD. Zakir Hossain, Ferdous Sohel, Mohd Fairuz Shiratuddin, and Hamid Laga. 2019. A comprehensive survey of deep learning for image captioning. *ACM Comput. Surv.*, 51(6).

Wentao Jiang, Ning Xu, Jiayun Wang, Chen Gao, Jing Shi, Zhe Lin, and Si Liu. 2021a. Language-guided global image editing via cross-modal cyclic mechanism. In *Proceedings of the IEEE/CVF International Conference on Computer Vision*, pages 2115–2124.

Yifan Jiang, Shiyu Chang, and Zhangyang Wang. 2021b. Transgan: Two transformers can make one strong GAN.

Adriana Kovashka, Devi Parikh, and Kristen Grauman. 2012. Whittlesearch: Image search with relative attribute feedback. In *2012 IEEE Conference on Computer Vision and Pattern Recognition*, pages 2973–2980. IEEE.

Yann LeCun, Bernhard Boser, John Denker, Donnie Henderson, Richard Howard, Wayne Hubbard, and Lawrence Jackel. 1989. Handwritten digit recognition with a back-propagation network. *Advances in neural information processing systems*, 2.

Kishore Papineni, Salim Roukos, Todd Ward, and Wei-Jing Zhu. 2002. Bleu: a method for automatic evaluation of machine translation. In *Proceedings of the 40th annual meeting of the Association for Computational Linguistics*, pages 311–318.

Alec Radford, Jong Wook Kim, Chris Hallacy, Aditya Ramesh, Gabriel Goh, Sandhini Agarwal, Girish Sastry, Amanda Askell, Pamela Mishkin, Jack Clark, et al. 2021. Learning transferable visual models from natural language supervision. *arXiv preprint arXiv:2103.00020*.

Alec Radford, Jeffrey Wu, Rewon Child, David Luan, Dario Amodei, Ilya Sutskever, et al. 2019. Language models are unsupervised multitask learners.

Aditya Ramesh, Prafulla Dhariwal, Alex Nichol, Casey Chu, and Mark Chen. 2022. Hierarchical text-conditional image generation with clip latents. *arXiv preprint arXiv:2204.06125*.

Aditya Ramesh, Mikhail Pavlov, Gabriel Goh, Scott Gray, Chelsea Voss, Alec Radford, Mark Chen, and Ilya Sutskever. 2021. Zero-shot text-to-image generation. *arXiv preprint arXiv:2102.12092*.

Scott Reed, Zeynep Akata, Xinchen Yan, Lajanugen Logeswaran, Bernt Schiele, and Honglak Lee. 2016. Generative adversarial text to image synthesis. In *International Conference on Machine Learning*, pages 1060–1069. PMLR.

Ming Tao, Hao Tang, Songsong Wu, Nicu Sebe, Xiao-Yuan Jing, Fei Wu, and Bingkun Bao. 2021. Df-gan: Deep fusion generative adversarial networks for text-to-image synthesis.

Ashish Vaswani, Noam Shazeer, Niki Parmar, Jakob Uszkoreit, Llion Jones, Aidan N Gomez, Łukasz Kaiser, and Illia Polosukhin. 2017. Attention is all you need. In *Advances in neural information processing systems*, pages 5998–6008.

Zhou Wang, Alan C Bovik, Hamid R Sheikh, and Eero P Simoncelli. 2004. Image quality assessment: from error visibility to structural similarity. *IEEE transactions on image processing*, 13(4):600–612.

Chenfei Wu, Jian Liang, Lei Ji, Fan Yang, Yuejian Fang, Daxin Jiang, and Nan Duan. 2021. NÜWA: Visual synthesis pre-training for neural visual world creation. *arXiv preprint arXiv:2111.12417*.

Qi Wu, Chunhua Shen, Peng Wang, Anthony Dick, and Anton Van Den Hengel. 2017. Image captioning and visual question answering based on attributes and external knowledge. *IEEE transactions on pattern analysis and machine intelligence*, 40(6):1367–1381.

Kelvin Xu, Jimmy Ba, Ryan Kiros, Kyunghyun Cho, Aaron Courville, Ruslan Salakhudinov, Rich Zemel, and Yoshua Bengio. 2015. Show, attend and tell: Neural image caption generation with visual attention. In *International conference on machine learning*, pages 2048–2057. PMLR.

Tao Xu, Pengchuan Zhang, Qiuyuan Huang, Han Zhang, Zhe Gan, Xiaolei Huang, and Xiaodong He. 2017. Attngan: Fine-grained text to image generation with attentional generative adversarial networks.

Aron Yu and Kristen Grauman. 2017. Fine-grained comparisons with attributes. In *Visual Attributes*, pages 119–154. Springer.

Tianhao Zhang, Hung-Yu Tseng, Lu Jiang, Weilong Yang, Honglak Lee, and Irfan Essa. 2021. Text as neural operator: Image manipulation by text instruction. In *Proceedings of the 29th ACM International Conference on Multimedia*, pages 1893–1902.

Jiapeng Zhu, Yujun Shen, Deli Zhao, and Bolei Zhou. 2020. In-domain gan inversion for real image editing. In *European conference on computer vision*, pages 592–608. Springer.

Minfeng Zhu, Pingbo Pan, Wei Chen, and Yi Yang. 2019. Dm-gan: Dynamic memory generative adversarial networks for text-to-image synthesis. *2019 IEEE/CVF Conference on Computer Vision and Pattern Recognition (CVPR)*, pages 5795–5803.

Peiye Zhuang, Oluwasanmi Koyejo, and Alexander G Schwing. 2021. Enjoy your editing: Controllable gans for image editing via latent space navigation. *arXiv preprint arXiv:2102.01187*.

A CIA Manual Evaluation Sheet

A.1 TEST A

First page of the test set A. Remaining pages can be consulted at https://github.com/nlx-group/LX-DRIM. From left to right: source image, generated image, and text snippet with alteration request.

		Are a lime green color	
		Are shiny grey clogs	
		Is white	
		Are metallic silver	
		Black flats	
		Is busier with contrasting panels and strap	

A.2 TEST B

First page of the test set B. Remaining pages can be consulted at https://github.com/nlx-group/LX-DRIM. From left to right: source image, target gold image, generated image, text snippet with alteration requested.

	Is plum, not black	
	Is gold	
	Is busier with laces and zipper with rugged sole	
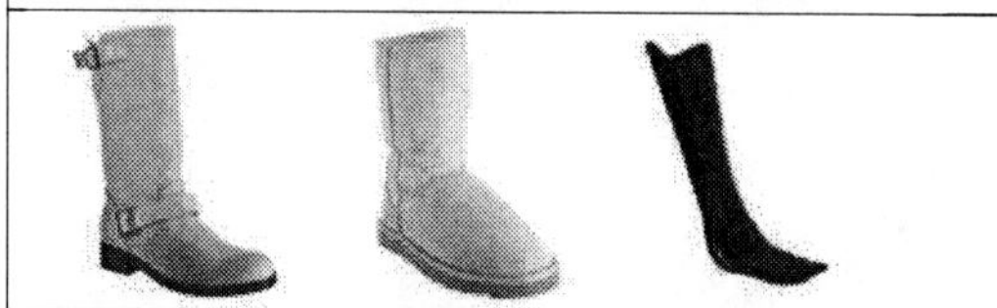	Have no heels	
	White sneakers with blue trim	
	Are yellow	
	Are blue and silver	

B CIG Manual Evaluation Sheet

First page of the CIG test set. Other pages can be consulted at https://github.com/nlx-group/LX-DRIM. From left to right: image caption, image generated by our system, image generated by DALL-E Mini.

ballet flats		
beige sneakers		
black flats with design		
black low heel motorcycle boot		
black mid-heeled long-on-the-leg boots		

Shapes of Emotions: Multimodal Emotion Recognition in Conversations via Emotion Shifts

Harsh Agarwal* **Keshav Bansal*** **Abhinav Joshi** **Ashutosh Modi**
Indian Institute of Technology Kanpur (IIT-K)
{harshagarwal0194,keshav22bansal}@gmail.com
{ajoshi,ashutoshm}@cse.iitk.ac.in

Abstract

Emotion Recognition in Conversations (ERC) is an important and active research area. Recent work has shown the benefits of using multiple modalities (e.g., text, audio, and video) for the ERC task. In a conversation, participants tend to maintain a particular emotional state unless some stimuli evokes a change. There is a continuous ebb and flow of emotions in a conversation. Inspired by this observation, we propose a multimodal ERC model and augment it with an emotion-shift component that improves performance. The proposed emotion-shift component is modular and can be added to any existing multimodal ERC model (with a few modifications). We experiment with different variants of the model, and results show that the inclusion of emotion shift signal helps the model to outperform existing models for ERC on MOSEI and IEMOCAP datasets.

1 Introduction

Humans are complex social beings, and emotions are indicative of not just their inner state and feelings but also their internal thinking process (Minsky, 2007). To fully understand a person, one needs to understand their inherent emotions. Recent research has witnessed colossal interest in including artificially intelligent machines as conversable companions for humans, e.g., personal digital assistants. However, communication with AI systems is quite limited. AI systems do not understand the inherent emotions expressed implicitly by humans making them unable to comprehend the underlying thought processes and respond appropriately. Consequently, a wide variety of approaches have been proposed for developing emotion understanding and generation systems (Sharma and Dhall, 2021; Witon et al., 2018; Singh et al., 2021a; Goswamy et al., 2020; Colombo et al., 2019; Singh et al., 2021b; Joshi et al., 2022).

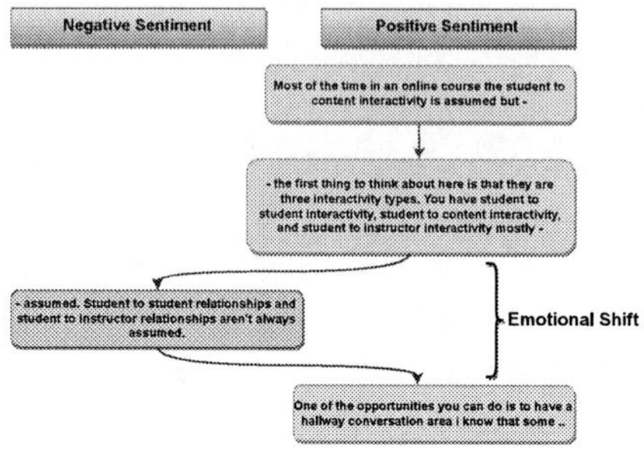

Figure 1: Emotional shift on the dialogue "m7SJs73SF8w" from CMU-MOSEI dataset

During an interaction, humans express different emotions and fluctuate between multiple emotional states. It is often the case that participants in a conversation tend to maintain a particular emotional state unless some stimuli evokes a change. This observation is closely related to *Shapes of Stories* proposed by renowned writer Kurt Vonnegut (Vonnegut, 1995), who posits that every story has a shape plotted by the ups and downs experienced by the characters of the story, and this, in turn, defines an *Emotional Arc* of a story. This phenomenon has also been empirically verified by Reagan et al. (2016), who analyzed around 1300 stories to come up with common emotional arc patterns across various stories. Moreover, apart from these flows, there exists a sudden shift of emotions from positive to negative sentiments. Consider an example shown in Figure 1, where the sentiment of the third utterance shifts from positive to negative and back again to positive in the fourth utterance. Current state-of-the-art methods are often oblivious to the presence of such emotion shifts and tend to fail in cases where there is a sudden change in the emotional state (Poria et al., 2019). To address this issue, we propose incorporating a novel module that explicitly tracks such emotional shifts in conversations. Humans express their emotions via various modalities, such as language, modulations in voice, facial expressions, and body gestures. In this paper, to

*Equal Contributions

Proceedings of the 29th International Conference on Computational Linguistics, pages 44–56
October 12–17, 2022.

fully and correctly recognize human emotions, we propose a multimodal emotion recognition system that utilizes language, audio, and video modalities. We propose a multimodal ERC model based on GRUs that fuses information from different modalities. An independent emotional shift component captures the emotion shift signal between consecutive utterances, allowing the model to forget past information in case of an emotional shift. We make the following contributions:

- We propose a new deep learning based multimodal emotion recognition model that captures information from text, audio, and video modalities. We release the model implementation and experiments code in the supplement.
- We propose a novel emotion shift network (modeled via a Siamese network) that guides the main emotion recognition system by providing information about possible emotion shifts or transitions. The proposed component is modular, it can be pretrained and added to any existing multi-modal ERC (with a few modifications) to improve emotion prediction.
- The proposed model is experimented on the two widely known multimodal emotion recognition datasets (MOSEI and IEMOCAP), and results show that emotional shift component helps to outperform some of the existing models. We perform detailed analysis and ablation studies of the model and show the contribution of different components. We analyse the performance of our model in the classification of utterances having a shift in emotion and compare this with previous models and report an improvement due to the use of emotion-shift information. We further examine how the internal GRU gates behave during emotion shifts.

2 Related Work

Emotion recognition using multiple modalities is an active area of research leading to the development of widely popular benchmark datasets, e.g., CMU-MOSEI (Bagher Zadeh et al., 2018), and IEMOCAP (Busso et al., 2008). Recent works have highlighted the crucial aspects of self, and interpersonal dependencies in the emotional dynamics of the conversations (Poria et al., 2019). Another essential feature is the role of the local and global context for emotion recognition systems. Some notable works like Dialogue RNN (Majumder et al., 2018b) try to capture these properties by modeling each speaker with a party state and the emotion of each utterance by an emotional state. Furthermore, a context state is maintained to model the global conversation context. Another work Multilogue-Net (Shenoy and Sardana, 2020) highlights the limitation of the fusion mechanism used in Dialogue RNN (Majumder et al., 2018b) and tries to solve it using a party, context, and emotion GRUs for each modality. It uses a pairwise attention mechanism proposed by (Ghosal et al., 2018) to fuse the emotion states for all the modalities effectively. However, DialogueRNN highlights the poor performance in predicting the emotions with the utterances where the emotion shifts from positive to negative sentiments. Our work considers the emotion shifts present in the dialogues and tries to leverage them for improving emotion recognition. Another line of work includes Transformer-Based Joint-Encoding (TBJE) (Delbrouck et al., 2020) that achieves the state-of-the-art results on the sentiment task for the MOSEI dataset using a multimodal transformer-based model for combining multiple modalities. However, in the emotion task, TBJE is outperformed by the Multilogue-Net model. The possible reason highlighted by the paper is the lack of context-awareness in the architecture, as TBJE neither uses the previous nor next utterance to predict the emotion for the current utterance. Some of the other works in multimodal emotion recognition include the Memory Fusion network (MFN) (Zadeh et al., 2018), which aligns multimodal sequences using multi-view gated memory, Graph-MFN (Bagher Zadeh et al., 2018) which uses Dynamic Fusion Graph (DFG) and learns to model the n-modal interactions dynamically, and bc-LSTM (Poria et al., 2017) which uses an LSTM-based model to capture contextual information. CESTa (Wang et al., 2020) captures the emotional consistency in the utterances using CRF model (Lafferty et al., 2001) for boosting the performance of emotion classification and comes close to our idea of leveraging emotion shifts.

3 Task and Corpus

Problem Definition: Consider a conversation having utterances $u_1, \ldots, u_N$. The task of Emotion Recognition in Conversation (ERC) is to predict the emotion (or sentiment) of each utterance u_t. We define an utterance to be a coherent piece of information (single or multiple sentences) con-

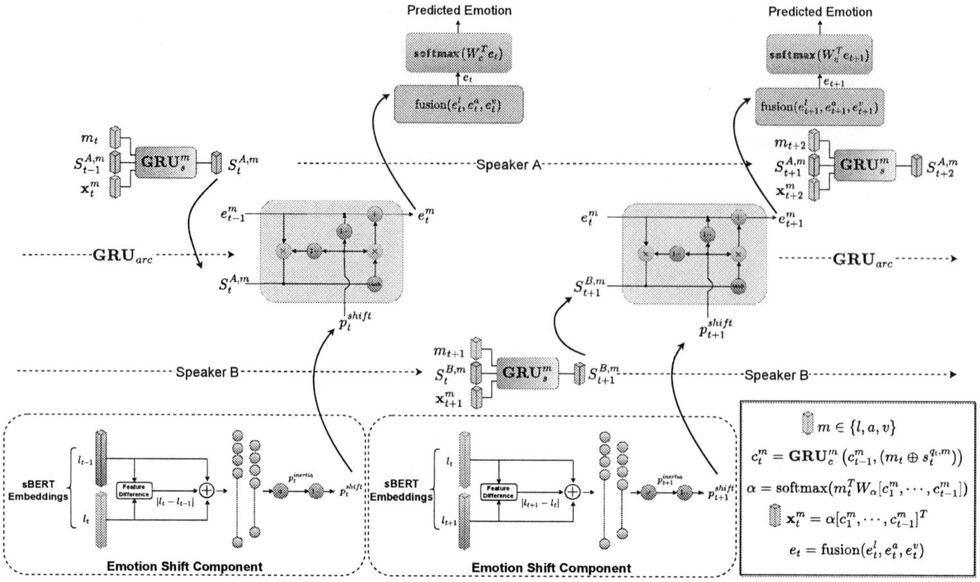

Figure 2: The model architecture for a conversation between two speakers, A and B, at time t and $t+1$. The upper part highlights the Emotion Classification Component, and the lower part highlights the Emotion Shift Component.

veyed by a single participant at a given time. We model an utterance in terms of different modalities: $u_t = \{l_t, a_t, v_t\}$. An utterance (u_t) at time-step t is represented via features from textual transcript (l_t), audio (a_t), and visuals (v_t) of the speaker. We denote the speaker of utterance u_t as q_t.

3.1 Corpus Details

3.1.1 CMU-MOSEI:

The CMU Multimodal Opinion Sentiment and Emotion Intensity (Bagher Zadeh et al., 2018) is an English language dataset containing more than 65 hours of annotated video from more than 10000 speakers and 250 topics. Each sentence is annotated for a sentiment on a $[-3, 3]$ Likert scale. However, in this work, we project these labels to a two-class classification setup with values ≥ 0 signifies positive sentiments and values < 0 convey negative sentiments. Dataset also contains six emotion labels, namely angry, happy, sad, surprise, fear and disgust for each utterance. Note that in case of emotions labels the utterances are multi-label. Which means a single utterance can have more than one emotion label. We have shown results for both sentiment and emotion prediction tasks.

3.1.2 IEMOCAP:

The IEMOCAP benchmark (Busso et al., 2008) consists of a conversation between ten distinct speakers. The dataset contains two-way conversations in videos where every video clip contains a single dyadic English dialogue. Further, each dialogue segments into utterances with an emotion label from six emotion labels, i.e., happy, sad, neutral, angry, excited, and frustrated. The dataset incorporates an acted setting where actors perform improvisations or scripted scenarios, specifically selected to elicit emotional expression.

4 The Proposed Model

During a conversation, speakers tend to maintain an emotional flow of affective states. These states majorly rely on the context of the entire conversation; for example, if the overall gist of the speaker about the topic is positive, the emotions like happiness, joy, and surprise can be seen more often than negative emotions like anger and sadness. Moreover, a speaker's emotions are often affected by the past emotions present in the conversation. Hence, an emotion prediction model should not only take into account the context but should also be able to maintain the speaker-level information along with the emotions present in the past utterances. Considering these assumptions, we propose the primary component of our emotion recognition model: the *Emotion Classification Component*. The emotions classification component predicts an utterance's emotion label using information from the current speaker, emotions of the previous utterances, and the entire conversation context. Another significant insight about the emotions in a conversation is the sudden shift of emotional states. Many of the existing state-of-the-art approaches highlight this in their error analysis, where the model fails to capture the sudden shifts in emotional states leading to a misclassified emotion prediction. To incorporate the effect of a sudden shift in the emotion, we introduce a separately trained component called the *Emotion Shift Component*. The emotion shift component explicitly models the probability (p_t^{shift}) of a shift in emotion between the utterances u_{t-1} and u_t. This shift in emotion can be expressed as moving from a positive (e.g., happy) to negative emotion (e.g., sad) or vice-versa between consecutive utterances. The emotion shift component being independent of the primary architecture is pretrained, and helps control the information flow from past to future during a sudden change. The signal from the pretrained emotional shift component is added to the emotion classification component to control the flow of emotions from past to future. Figure 2 shows detailed architecture of the proposed model.

Emotion Classification Component: For modeling the underlying emotions in a conversation, we maintain a *party state*, *emotion state* and *context state*. The party state is maintained for each speaker and helps to keep track of the participant specific aspect in a conversation. The context state is global (common across each participant) and helps to encode the entire conversation context, thereby capturing inter-utterance dependencies. Akin to the context state, the emotion state is also global and helps to leverage the emotion information flow between utterances. Moreover, the emotion shift signal between the current and previous utterance is used to update the global emotion state. The emotion label for each utterance is then predicted by decoding the emotion state. In our model each of the party, context and emotion states are modality specific and are updated using a modality specific GRU (Chung et al., 2014) network for each modality $m \in \{l, a, v\}$ (indicated by the superscript m). We employ late fusion to combine the emotion states from different modalities. Next, we explain different GRU networks used in the model.

$$s_t^{q_t,m} = \mathbf{GRU}_s^m \left(s_{t-1}^{q_t,m}, (m_t \oplus \mathbf{x}_t^m)\right) \quad (1)$$

$$c_t^m = \mathbf{GRU}_c^m \left(c_{t-1}^m, (m_t \oplus s_t^{q_t,m})\right) \quad (2)$$

$$e_t^m = \mathbf{GRU}_{arc}^m \left(e_{t-1}^m, s_t^{q_t,m}, p_t^{\text{shift}}\right) \quad (3)$$

$$e_t = \text{fusion}(e_t^l, e_t^a, e_t^v) \quad (4)$$

Party State Update (GRU_s): The state of each participant is modeled by the party state update GRU_s. For each modality $m \in \{l, a, v\}$, q_t's party state $s_{t-1}^{q_t,m}$ is updated to $s_t^{q_t,m}$ using an attention vector $\mathbf{x}_t^m$ and modality specific feature m_t (Eq. 1), $\oplus$ denotes concatenation operation. Here $\mathbf{x}_t^m$ is calculated using a simple dot product attention mechanism over the context states (c_t^m). Note that for all speakers other than q_t, the party state at $t-1$ and t remains the same.

Context State Update (GRU_c): Global conversation context is modeled using the context state update GRU_c. For each modality $m \in \{l, a, v\}$, the global context state c_{t-1}^m is updated to c_t^m (Eq. 2) using the q_t's party state $s_t^{q_t,m}$ and the corresponding modality feature m_t. Context states $(c_1^m, \cdots, c_{t-1}^m)$ are used for calculating the attention vector x_t^m for each modality $m \in \{l, a, v\}$ as follows:

$$\alpha = \text{softmax}\left(m_t^T W_\alpha \left[c_1^m, \cdots, c_{t-1}^m\right]\right) \quad (5)$$

$$x_t^m = \alpha \left[c_1^m, \cdots, c_{t-1}^m\right]^T \quad (6)$$

Emotion State Update (GRU_{arc}): For each modality $m \in \{l, a, v\}$, the global emotion state e_{t-1}^m is updated to e_t^m (Eq. 3) using the current party state $s_t^{q_t,m}$ and modulated by the emotion shift component (p_t^{shift}). The emotion states for all the three modalities are fused together (Eq. 4) to create e_t using a pairwise attention mechanism (Shenoy and Sardana, 2020). e_t is later used to decode the emotion class for an utterance.

The emotion classification component is a context-aware model similar to that of previous works like Multilogue-net (Shenoy and Sardana, 2020) but with a few key differences. Firstly, instead of modelling an emotion state for each participant, we introduce global emotion state for each conversation. This is done to make use of the flow of emotion between utterances. Secondly, the emotion shift signal between the current and previous utterance (p_t^{shift}) is used to update the global emotion state using a GRU_{arc} which aims to model the emotion arc in the conversation.

Emotion Shift Component: To capture the emotional arc across the conversation, we explicitly model probability of emotion shift (p_t^{shift}) between successive utterances (u_{t-1} and u_t). We use a Siamese network (Bromley et al., 1993) to model the emotional shift present across utterances. A Siamese network generally consists of two or more identical subnetworks having the same configuration with shared parameters and weights. The proposed emotion shift architecture takes the textual features of the current (l_t) and previous (l_{t-1}) utterances and outputs the probability of maintaining emotional inertia ($p_t^{inertia}$). The architecture of the emotion shift prediction network is shown in lower half of Figure 2. We use Sentence-BERT (SBERT) (Reimers and Gurevych, 2019) embeddings as textual features. SBERT is a modification of the pretrained BERT (Devlin et al., 2019) network that uses the Siamese network to derive semantically meaningful sentence embeddings for transfer learning tasks. The emotion shift prediction network makes use of only the text modality for two reasons. Firstly, it has often been found empirically that among the text, audio, and video modalities, text modality carries more information for ERC tasks (Poria et al., 2018). Secondly, early fusion techniques to combine the three modalities can suffer in a Siamese-type architecture due to difficulty in mapping the fused modality vector to a vector space in which similar vectors are close. We also experimentally verify this (§6).

The emotion shift prediction network (between u_t and u_{t-1}) takes in text features corresponding to utterances (l_t and l_{t-1}) and their element wise differences to output the probability of a shift as given by (Eq. 7). Here, $p_t^{inertia}$ is calculated using Siamese network (Eq. 8, 9). Here, $\mathcal{H}_t$ is the Siamese hidden state, $\mathcal{W}$ $\left(\in \mathbb{R}^{3d_l}\right)$ is the model parameter. For the Siamese network, we use Binary Cross Entropy loss ($\mathcal{L}_s$) over the distribution p_t^{shift}. The emotion shift component modulates the Emotion State GRU$_{arc}$ via p_t^{shift} and hence controls the flow of information during the conversation. The Emotion Shift component captures the emotional consistency in the utterances and can act as an independent modular component that can be pretrained and added to any existing multi-modal ERC framework with a few modifications for improving emotion recognition in conversations.

$$p_t^{\text{shift}} = 1 - p_t^{inertia} \tag{7}$$

$$p_t^{inertia} = \sigma\left(\mathcal{H}_t\right) \tag{8}$$

$$\mathcal{H}_t = \mathcal{W}^T (l_{t-1} \oplus l_t \oplus |l_t - l_{t-1}|) \tag{9}$$

Overall Architecture: The motivation for the proposed architecture follows from the intuition that we need to weigh down the contribution of the previous emotion state in case of an emotion shift. In other words, we need to reduce the influence of e_{t-1}^m in the calculation of e_t^m when there is a high p_t^{shift}. To do so, we modify the reset and update gates in the GRU modelling the emotional arc of the conversation i.e. GRU$_{arc}$. A GRU has gating units (reset and update gates) that modulate the flow of information inside the unit. Ravanelli et al. (2017) mention the usefulness of reset gate in scenarios where significant discontinuities are present in the sequence, thereby indicating its crucial role to forget information. Their work also finds a redundancy in the activations of the reset and update gates when processing speech sequences. Motivated by this, and the intuition that we need to forget more information when there is a higher probability of an emotional shift, we directly use the value of $(1 - p_t^{shift})$ for both the reset and update gates. The updates for GRU$_{arc}$ unit are given by Eqs. 10, 11. Eq. 10 calculates a candidate emotion state $\tilde{e}_t^m$ in which the prior emotion state's (e_{t-1}^m) is controlled by the emotion shift signal. The output e_t^m is a linear interpolation between $\tilde{e}_{t-1}^m$ and e_{t-1}^m. Again, p_t^{shift} controls the influence of e_{t-1}^m (Eq. 11). Therefore, a higher value of p_t^{shift} will limit the contribution of the previous emotion state. In the absence of the emotion shift component, the GRU gates are learned using only the classification data, much like the rest of the parameters in the model. If the total number of parameters in a model is huge (as is the case with most deep learning models), the gates might be unable to learn well. We verify that the modeling of the shift in emotion encourages better learning of these gates (§6).

$$\tilde{e}_t^m = \tanh\left(W s_t^{q_t,m} + (1 - p_t^{shift}) \odot \left(U e_{t-1}^m\right)\right) \tag{10}$$

$$e_t^m = (1 - p_t^{shift}) \odot e_{t-1}^m + p_t^{shift} \odot \tilde{e}_t^m \tag{11}$$

For prediction at time t, the emotion vector e_t (formed from fusion of e_t^m as described in (Eq. 4)) is passed through a final classification layer W_c ($\in \mathbb{R}^{d_e \times K}$) where K is the number of emotion or sentiment classes. This is used to obtain probability distribution over emotion labels via the Softmax activation: $o = \text{softmax}(W_c^T e_t)$. We use the Cross-Entropy Loss over this distribution to train the weights of the emotion classification component.

5 Experiments and Results

Multimodal Emotion Corpora: We evaluate our model using two benchmark English ERC datasets - CMU Multimodal Opinion Sentiment and Emotion

Dataset	#utterances		Emotion shift (in %)	
	Train	Test	Train	Test
CMU-MOSEI	18191	4655	33.61	34.62
IEMOCAP	5810	1623	12.89	12.75

Table 1: Statistics for number of utterances and emotion shift percentage in various datasets

Model	F1	Accuracy
Graph-MFN	77.00	76.90
DialogueRNN	79.82	79.98
Multilogue-Net	80.01	82.10
TBJE	-	82.4
Our Model	**83.07**	**82.66**

Table 2: Performance comparison on the sentiment task of CMU-MOSEI dataset (all numbers in %)

Emotion	Multilogue-Net		TBJE		Our Model	
	A	F1	A	F1	A	F1
Happiness	**70.05**	**70.03**	66.00	65.50	68.51	68.61
Sadness	71.04	70.42	73.90	67.90	**74.20**	**71.74**
Anger	74.78	74.31	**81.90**	76.00	75.17	**76.10**
Disgust	77.98	79.20	**86.50**	**84.50**	83.67	82.79
Fear	69.04	75.50	**89.20**	**87.20**	87.11	85.90
Surprise	88.89	85.98	**90.60**	**86.10**	78.99	81.62

Table 3: Performance comparison on the emotion task of CMU-MOSEI dataset (all numbers in %)

Intensity (CMU-MOSEI) dataset and the Interactive Emotional Dyadic Motion Capture (IEMOCAP) dataset. Details of these corpora are discussed in §3.1. In a nutshell, each of the two corpora has language, audio, and video modalities. MOSEI has both sentiment and six emotion labels, IEMOCAP has video recordings of dyadic conversations and is labeled with six emotion labels.

Emotion shift in Dataset: We define an emotion shift between consecutive utterances if there is a shift from a positive to a negative emotion or vice-versa. CMU-MOSEI dataset provides annotated (positive/negative) sentiment label for each utterance. This is not the case for the IEMOCAP dataset, therefore we divide the emotion classes into a positive and negative category. Happiness and surprise are taken into the positive category while disgust, angry and sad are considered as the negative category. Note that IEMOCAP also has a neutral emotion, but a shift is only counted if it is from a positive to negative emotion or vice-versa. Table 1 shows the percentage of emotion shift observed in the datasets. Since CMU-MOSEI shows a larger amount of emotion shift, we were motivated to perform experiments on CMU-MOSEI first.

5.1 Results

We evaluate our approaches using standard F1 score and Accuracy evaluation metrics (App. A). We train and report the performance of our model for four sub-tasks, 2-way sentiment classification and binary emotion classification on CMU-MOSEI, and four-class and six-class emotion classification task for IEMOCAP. The focus of our work is multimodal ERC and consequently, as is done in previous work, we compare only with previous multimodal approaches, since comparison with unimodal (e.g., text) only approaches does not make sense. Moreover, SOTA unimodal approaches (such as text based) use additional information such external knowledge sources (e.g., (Ghosal et al., 2020)) which makes the comparison with multimodal approach unfair specially given that such knowledge may not be available for other modalities. Nevertheless, it is possible to incorporate the emotion shift component into existing emotion prediction architectures (unimodal or multimodal) and we leave this exploration for future.

Results on CMU-MOSEI: Table 2 shows comparison of our best performing model on CMU-MOSEI sentiment labels, with current state of the art models: TBJE (Delbrouck et al., 2020), Multilogue-Net (Shenoy and Sardana, 2020), Dialogue RNN (Majumder et al., 2018b), and Graph-MFN (Poria et al., 2017). As evident from the results, we are able to significantly outperform the previous SOTA Multilogue-Net model with an increase of 3% in F1 score. We further compare our model on the emotion classification task with TBJE and Multilogue-Net (Table 3). As shown in the table, our model outperforms for some of the emotion classes. We speculate that poor performance is due to the multilabel setting in the CMU-MOSEI dataset. As the emotion labels are multilabel, the emotion shift component is not able to play a meaningful role in providing a performance boost to the emotion classification component. We consider multilabel settings as another line of future work where the emotion shift modeling takes into account the multilabel property.

Results on IEMOCAP: Previous works on Multimodal-IEMOCAP have shown performance only on angry, happy, sad, and neutral emotions. We compare our model performance on these four classes with state-of-the-art models CHFusion (Majumder et al., 2018a) and bc-LSTM (Poria et al.,

Emotion	bc-LSTM		CHFusion		Our model	
	A	F1	A	F1	A	F1
Happy	**79.31**	-	74.30	**81.40**	68.75	72.79
Sad	**78.30**	-	75.60	77.00	76.73	**81.21**
Neutral	69.92	-	78.40	71.20	**81.51**	**78.25**
Angry	77.98	-	79.60	77.60	**82.35**	**79.77**
Avg(w)	75.20	-	76.50	76.80	**78.47**	**78.46**

Table 4: Performance comparison on the IEMOCAP dataset for four emotion labels (all numbers in %)

Emotion	Hap	Sad	Neu	Ang	Exc	Fru	Avg(w)
Acc	54.17	65.31	62.50	62.94	67.89	64.04	63.59
F1	50.81	70.48	60.23	63.69	70.73	62.72	63.82

Table 5: Performance of our model on IEMOCAP dataset for 6 labels (all numbers in %)

2017) (Table 4). Our model significantly outperforms both of these on average weighted F1 and Accuracy. Also, emotion classes neutral and angry show improved performance. We also provide results on six emotion classes - happy, sad, neutral, angry, excited, and frustrated (Table 5). For these experiments, we use BERT features for text (§6), OpenSmile features for audio and 3D-CNN features (Majumder et al., 2018b) for video. We did not come across any existing work on 6-class multimodal IEMOCAP for the comparison.

Performance of emotion shift component: The results describing the capability of the emotion shift component to predict the shift for CMU-MOSEI and IEMOCAP dataset are shown in Table 6. It is to be noted that predicting the shift accurately is not our primary objective. Our objective is to be able to improve the emotion prediction by using the signal (p_t^{shift}) received from the emotion shift component.

6 Analysis and Ablation Studies

Due to a wide variety of components, it becomes vital to perform a detailed analysis of the architecture to understand the importance of various choices.

Feature and Design choices: For understanding the importance of features used for different modalities, we choose two different sets of features for text and visual modalities. In one setting, we use averaged GloVe embeddings (Pennington et al., 2014) for text, OpenSmile features (Eyben et al., 2010) for Audio and Facet features (Stöckli et al., 2017) for Video. Whereas in another setting, for text modality, we make use of a pre-trained BERT (Devlin et al., 2019) model's output layer. We calculate the average of the output layer to get a fixed-sized

Datasets		Accuracy	F1
CMU-MOSEI		72.65	67.32
IEMOCAP	4-label	80.50	79.68
	6-label	85.63	84.28

Table 6: Performance of Siamese Model on MOSEI and IEMOCAP

Input Features	Classification		Emotion Shift	
	Accuracy	F1	Accuracy	F1
G(L), O(A), F(V)	80.85	80.31	63.38	62.15
B(L), O(A), O(V)	81.98	80.91	64.01	63.30
B(L), O(A), O(V)	**82.66**	**83.07**	**72.65**	**67.32**

Table 7: Effect of different feature combinations for MOSEI. The classification columns are results on 2 class sentiment prediction task and emotion shift columns are results on 2 class emotion shifts classes. Here G(L): Glove, B(L): BERT, F(V): Facet, O(A): OpenSmile, O(V): OpenFace2.0

vector. For visual modality, we use the features provided by OpenFace2.0 (Baltrusaitis et al., 2018), which are useful in performing facial analysis tasks such as facial landmark detection, head-pose tracking, and eye-gaze tracking. The results in Table 7 (first two rows) highlight the advantage of features used in second setting.

Importance of Pretraining the Emotion Shift Component: To review the significance of the pretraining emotion shift component, we compare it with the two settings described above. We argue that jointly optimizing the emotion classification and emotion shift component from scratch might degrade the model classification performance. At the onset of training, the Siamese component does not provide a helpful signal to the classification component due to the random initialization of its weights, hampering the learning of the classification component. To prevent this, we pre-train the emotion shift component on the emotion shift labels separately before the joint training task, which helps provide the classification component with a better emotion shift signal at the start of training, making learning more accessible. The results in Table 7 (third row) shows an increase of approximately 2% in the F1 score when compared to the same features setting without pretraining (second row). Moreover, the Siamese network, when pretrained, also achieves an F1 score of 67.32%, the highest among all the experiments depicting the hindrance caused by joint training from scratch.

Performance over emotion shift utterances: To verify the effectiveness of the emotion shift com-

Emotion shift type	Multilogue-Net	Our Model
Positive - Negative	69.78	**73.83**
Negative - Positive	59.49	**80.35**

Table 8: Accuracy comparison with Multilogue-Net on MOSEI emotion shift utterances

Emotion shift type	4-label	6-label
Positive - Negative	63.04	53.22
Negative - Positive	69.77	70.68

Table 9: Accuracy of the proposed model on IEMOCAP emotion shift utterances

ponent we consider cases where an emotion shift has occurred between a target utterance u_t and the prior utterance u_{t-1} if there is a switch from positive emotion in u_{t-1} to negative emotion in u_t, or vice versa (§3). We evaluate our emotion classification performance on such utterances u_t displaying an emotion shift. Popular architectures like CMN, ICON, IANN and DialogueRNN perform poorly on the utterances with an emotion shift (Poria et al., 2019). In particular, in cases where the emotion of the target utterance differs from the previous utterance, DialogueRNN could only correctly predict 47.5% instances, much lesser than the 69.2% success rate that it achieves at the regions of no emotional shift. In Table 8 we compare our results with another multimodal ERC SOTA: Multilogue-Net. The results show a significant increase in accuracy for both positive to negative and negative to positive emotion shifts on the CMU-MOSEI dataset depicting the importance of the independent emotion shift component introduced in our architecture. Even though the Siamese network can predict the presence of emotion shift with an accuracy of about 72.65% (Table 7), the signal received from it (in the form of reset and update gates of GRU) helps the emotion classification network to overcome the emotional inertia and predict the correct emotion. We also show the accuracy of our model on emotion shift utterances of the IEMOCAP dataset in Table 9. We could not calculate these numbers for CHFusion (SOTA on IEMOCAP) due unavailability of their code.

Effect of Modeling Emotion Shift: To further verify the significance of modeling emotion shift as a separate component, we compare two variants of our best model - one with and the other without the Emotion shift component. Table 10 shows a comparison on both the datasets. Across both the

Datasets		Without		With	
		A	F1	A	F1
CMU-MOSEI		81.31	81.01	**82.66**	**83.07**
IEMOCAP	4-label	77.53	77.51	**78.47**	**78.46**
	6-label	61.37	61.65	**66.73**	**66.86**

Table 10: Performance with and without the emotion shift component (all numbers in %)

Datasets		L+A		L+V		A+V		L+A+V	
		A	F1	A	F1	A	F1	A	F1
CMU-MOSEI		82.49	82.81	81.65	82.16	72.22	71.28	**82.66**	**83.07**
IEMOCAP	4-label	**80.06**	**80.07**	77.52	77.56	78.26	78.20	78.47	78.46
	6-label	64.26	64.48	63.34	63.40	58.90	58.84	**66.73**	**66.86**

Table 11: Ablation study to observe the contribution of different modalities

datasets, we observe a substantial increase in performance while using the emotion shift component.

Contributions of the Modalities: To understand the importance of different modalities present in the datasets, we conduct experiments by choosing a combination of two out of the three modalities. As expected, models using all three modalities outperform models using only two modalities across most datasets (Table 11). On the IEMOCAP dataset with four classes, the text+audio model performs better than six classes. The text modality seems to be the most essential compared to other modalities highlighting the significance of context.

Using other modalities in the Emotion Shift Component: To observe the effectiveness of modalities other than text on the Emotion Shift Component, we empirically analyze the effect of using all three modalities for training this component. We make use of the early fusion technique where modalities l_t, a_t, v_t are concatenated ($l_t \oplus a_t \oplus v_t$) and then passed to the Siamese network. Observing the obtained results, we see that the use of the three modalities does not lead to an improvement (Table 12). A possible reason for this might be the importance of context (captured in the text modality) in predicting emotion shifts.

Analyzing reset gate updates in GRU$_{arc}$: We also verify the practical significance of the emotion shift component qualitatively. We compare the GRU reset gate activations obtained from the emotion shift component and the reset gate activations learned by GRU without explicit emotion shift information. We randomly pick an instance from the CMU-MOSEI test set and analyze the GRU unit using it. In Figure 3, we show these activations for the Video ID "m7SJs73SF8w" randomly selected

Modalities	Accuracy	F1
L	**82.66**	**83.07**
L+A+V	82.20	82.78

Table 12: Performance using other modalities in Siamese component (all numbers in %)

from the test set. This dialogue has four utterances, and we see a shift from positive to negative emotion between utterances two and three and a shift from negative to positive emotion between utterances three and four. As seen in the left graph in Figure 3, the emotion shift component learns to set a low reset gate value when there is an emotion shift (namely timestamps $t = 3$ and $t = 4$). This low reset gate value helps to weigh down the contribution of the previous emotion state for the predictions at the current timestamp. Comparing it to the case when we remove the emotion shift component (right graph in Figure 3), the reset gate activations learned by the GRU do not follow the same trend, indicating that the previous emotion state will still significantly contribute to predictions at the current timestamp. Overall, the emotion shift component plays a vital role in effectively controlling information from the past.

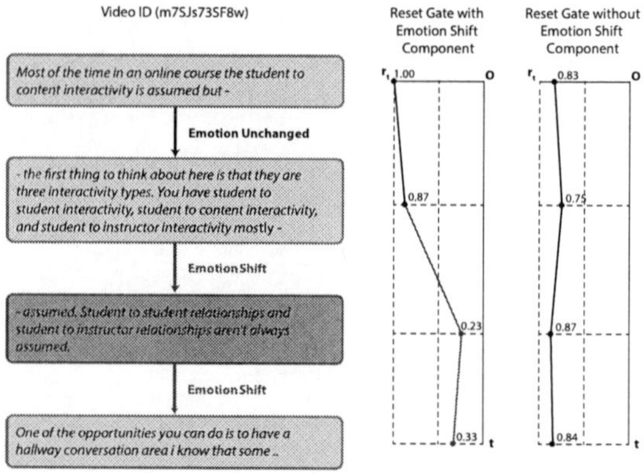

Figure 3: Reset Gate activations on the dialogue 'm7SJs73SF8w" from CMU-MOSEI test dataset

7 Discussion

The presence of emotion shifts in human-to-human conversation is prominent in the conversational datasets. The existing works based on sequential modeling often suffer from these shifts, leading to poor performance for utterances with emotion shifts. In this work, we try to control the effect of previous utterances using an independent emotion shift module. As highlighted in Tables 8 and 9, the proposed architecture performs significantly better on emotion shift cases when compared to Multilogue-Net (20% improvement in negative-positive and 4% improvement on positive-negative shifts). The novel design of the emotion shift-based gating mechanism in the GRU unit helps boost the prediction performance for utterances with emotion shifts. As noticed in Fig. 3, the reset and update gates provide a significant signal when there is an emotional shift in conversation.

Modularity: The modular design and idea of the proposed emotion shift component can further be used to improve any emotion prediction systems that have poor performance in emotion shift cases. Moreover, the designed emotion shift component works considering only the textual modality, making it applicable to both multimodal as well as unimodal systems.

Application to Real-Time Systems: A notable limitation of all the existing Emotion Recognition state-of-the-art systems often comes from the incapability of their implementations for real-time use cases as they require the entire context to be given in the form of multiple utterances to the model. For future approaches where the models will target the real-time setting, the proposed emotion shift component can be handy as it only uses two consecutive utterances to predict the emotion shift.

8 Conclusion and Future Directions

In this paper, we proposed a deep learning based model for multimodal emotion recognition in conversations. We proposed a new emotion shift component (modeled using the Siamese net) that captures the emotional arc in a conversation and steers the main emotion recognition model. We performed a battery of experiments on two main emotion recognition datasets. Results and analysis show the importance of the emotion shift component. Currently, the emotion shift component uses only the text modality for predicting the shift and we plan to explore more sophisticated ways of using information from multiple modalities.

9 Acknowledgements

We would like to thank reviewers for their insightful comments. This research is supported by SERB India (Science and Engineering Board) Research Grant number SRG/2021/000768.

References

AmirAli Bagher Zadeh, Paul Pu Liang, Soujanya Poria, Erik Cambria, and Louis-Philippe Morency. 2018. Multimodal language analysis in the wild: CMU-MOSEI dataset and interpretable dynamic fusion graph. In *Proceedings of the 56th Annual Meeting of the Association for Computational Linguistics (Volume 1: Long Papers)*, pages 2236–2246, Melbourne, Australia. Association for Computational Linguistics.

Tadas Baltrusaitis, Amir Zadeh, Yao Chong Lim, and Louis-Philippe Morency. 2018. Openface 2.0: Facial behavior analysis toolkit. In *2018 13th IEEE International Conference on Automatic Face Gesture Recognition (FG 2018)*.

Jane Bromley, J.W. Bentz, Leon Bottou, I. Guyon, Yann Lecun, C. Moore, Eduard Sackinger, and R. Shah. 1993. Signature verification using a siamese time delay neural network. *International Journal of Pattern Recognition and Artificial Intelligence*, 7(4).

Lars Buitinck, Gilles Louppe, Mathieu Blondel, Fabian Pedregosa, Andreas Mueller, Olivier Grisel, Vlad Niculae, Peter Prettenhofer, Alexandre Gramfort, Jaques Grobler, Robert Layton, Jake VanderPlas, Arnaud Joly, Brian Holt, and Gaël Varoquaux. 2013. API design for machine learning software: experiences from the scikit-learn project. In *ECML PKDD Workshop: Languages for Data Mining and Machine Learning*, pages 108–122.

Carlos Busso, Murtaza Bulut, Chi-Chun Lee, Abe Kazemzadeh, Emily Mower Provost, Samuel Kim, Jeannette Chang, Sungbok Lee, and Shrikanth Narayanan. 2008. Iemocap: Interactive emotional dyadic motion capture database. *Language Resources and Evaluation*, 42:335–359.

Junyoung Chung, Caglar Gulcehre, KyungHyun Cho, and Yoshua Bengio. 2014. Empirical evaluation of gated recurrent neural networks on sequence modeling. *arXiv preprint arXiv:1412.3555*.

Pierre Colombo, Wojciech Witon, Ashutosh Modi, James Kennedy, and Mubbasir Kapadia. 2019. Affect-driven dialog generation. *arXiv preprint arXiv:1904.02793*.

Jean-Benoit Delbrouck, Noé Tits, Mathilde Brousmiche, and Stéphane Dupont. 2020. A transformer-based joint-encoding for emotion recognition and sentiment analysis. In *Second Grand-Challenge and Workshop on Multimodal Language (Challenge-HML)*, pages 1–7, Seattle, USA. Association for Computational Linguistics.

Jacob Devlin, Ming-Wei Chang, Kenton Lee, and Kristina Toutanova. 2019. Bert: Pre-training of deep bidirectional transformers for language understanding.

Florian Eyben, Martin Wöllmer, and Björn Schuller. 2010. opensmile – the munich versatile and fast open-source audio feature extractor. In *MM'10 - Proceedings of the ACM Multimedia 2010 International Conference*, pages 1459–1462.

Deepanway Ghosal, Md Shad Akhtar, Dushyant Chauhan, Soujanya Poria, Asif Ekbal, and Pushpak Bhattacharyya. 2018. Contextual inter-modal attention for multi-modal sentiment analysis. In *Proceedings of the 2018 Conference on Empirical Methods in Natural Language Processing*, pages 3454–3466, Brussels, Belgium. Association for Computational Linguistics.

Deepanway Ghosal, Navonil Majumder, Alexander Gelbukh, Rada Mihalcea, and Soujanya Poria. 2020. Cosmic: Commonsense knowledge for emotion identification in conversations.

Tushar Goswamy, Ishika Singh, Ahsan Barkati, and Ashutosh Modi. 2020. Adapting a language model for controlled affective text generation. In *Proceedings of the 28th International Conference on Computational Linguistics*, pages 2787–2801.

Abhinav Joshi, Ashwani Bhat, Ayush Jain, Atin Singh, and Ashutosh Modi. 2022. COGMEN: COntextualized GNN based multimodal emotion recognitioN. In *Proceedings of the 2022 Conference of the North American Chapter of the Association for Computational Linguistics: Human Language Technologies*, pages 4148–4164, Seattle, United States. Association for Computational Linguistics.

Diederik Kingma and Jimmy Ba. 2014. Adam: A method for stochastic optimization. *International Conference on Learning Representations*.

John D. Lafferty, Andrew McCallum, and Fernando C. N. Pereira. 2001. Conditional random fields: Probabilistic models for segmenting and labeling sequence data. In *Proceedings of the Eighteenth International Conference on Machine Learning*, ICML '01, page 282–289, San Francisco, CA, USA. Morgan Kaufmann Publishers Inc.

Navonil Majumder, Devamanyu Hazarika, Alexander F. Gelbukh, Erik Cambria, and Soujanya Poria. 2018a. Multimodal sentiment analysis using hierarchical fusion with context modeling. *CoRR*, abs/1806.06228.

Navonil Majumder, Soujanya Poria, Devamanyu Hazarika, Rada Mihalcea, Alexander F. Gelbukh, and Erik Cambria. 2018b. Dialoguernn: An attentive RNN for emotion detection in conversations. *CoRR*, abs/1811.00405.

Marvin Minsky. 2007. *The emotion machine: Commonsense thinking, artificial intelligence, and the future of the human mind.* Simon and Schuster.

Adam Paszke, Sam Gross, Francisco Massa, Adam Lerer, James Bradbury, Gregory Chanan, Trevor Killeen, Zeming Lin, Natalia Gimelshein, Luca Antiga, Alban Desmaison, Andreas Köpf, Edward Yang, Zach DeVito, Martin Raison, Alykhan Tejani,

Sasank Chilamkurthy, Benoit Steiner, Lu Fang, Junjie Bai, and Soumith Chintala. 2019. Pytorch: An imperative style, high-performance deep learning library.

Jeffrey Pennington, Richard Socher, and Christopher Manning. 2014. GloVe: Global vectors for word representation. In *Proceedings of the 2014 Conference on Empirical Methods in Natural Language Processing (EMNLP)*, pages 1532–1543, Doha, Qatar. Association for Computational Linguistics.

Soujanya Poria, Erik Cambria, Devamanyu Hazarika, Navonil Majumder, Amir Zadeh, and Louis-Philippe Morency. 2017. Context-dependent sentiment analysis in user-generated videos. In *Proceedings of the 55th Annual Meeting of the Association for Computational Linguistics (Volume 1: Long Papers)*, pages 873–883, Vancouver, Canada. Association for Computational Linguistics.

Soujanya Poria, Navonil Majumder, Devamanyu Hazarika, Erik Cambria, Amir Hussain, and Alexander F. Gelbukh. 2018. Multimodal sentiment analysis: Addressing key issues and setting up baselines. *CoRR*, abs/1803.07427.

Soujanya Poria, Navonil Majumder, Rada Mihalcea, and Eduard H. Hovy. 2019. Emotion recognition in conversation: Research challenges, datasets, and recent advances. *CoRR*, abs/1905.02947.

Mirco Ravanelli, Philemon Brakel, Maurizio Omologo, and Yoshua Bengio. 2017. Improving speech recognition by revising gated recurrent units. *CoRR*, abs/1710.00641.

Andrew J Reagan, Lewis Mitchell, Dilan Kiley, Christopher M Danforth, and Peter Sheridan Dodds. 2016. The emotional arcs of stories are dominated by six basic shapes. *EPJ Data Science*, 5(1):1–12.

Nils Reimers and Iryna Gurevych. 2019. Sentence-bert: Sentence embeddings using siamese bert-networks.

Garima Sharma and Abhinav Dhall. 2021. A survey on automatic multimodal emotion recognition in the wild. In *Advances in Data Science: Methodologies and Applications*, pages 35–64. Springer.

Aman Shenoy and Ashish Sardana. 2020. Multiloguenet: A context-aware rnn for multi-modal emotion detection and sentiment analysis in conversation. *Second Grand-Challenge and Workshop on Multimodal Language (Challenge-HML)*.

Aaditya Singh, Shreeshail Hingane, Saim Wani, and Ashutosh Modi. 2021a. An end-to-end network for emotion-cause pair extraction. In *Proceedings of the Eleventh Workshop on Computational Approaches to Subjectivity, Sentiment and Social Media Analysis*, pages 84–91, Online. Association for Computational Linguistics.

Gargi Singh, Dhanajit Brahma, Piyush Rai, and Ashutosh Modi. 2021b. Fine-grained emotion prediction by modeling emotion definitions. In *2021 9th International Conference on Affective Computing and Intelligent Interaction (ACII)*, pages 1–8. IEEE.

Sabrina Stöckli, Michael Schulte-Mecklenbeck, Stefan Borer, and Andrea Samson. 2017. Facial expression analysis with affdex and facet: A validation study. *Behavior Research Methods*, 50.

Kurt Vonnegut. 1995. Shapes of stories. *Vonnegut's Shapes of Stories*.

Yan Wang, Jiayu Zhang, Jun Ma, Shaojun Wang, and Jing Xiao. 2020. Contextualized emotion recognition in conversation as sequence tagging. In *Proceedings of the 21th Annual Meeting of the Special Interest Group on Discourse and Dialogue*, pages 186–195, 1st virtual meeting. Association for Computational Linguistics.

Wojciech Witon, Pierre Colombo, Ashutosh Modi, and Mubbasir Kapadia. 2018. Disney at iest 2018: Predicting emotions using an ensemble. In *Proceedings of the 9th Workshop on Computational Approaches to Subjectivity, Sentiment and Social Media Analysis*, pages 248–253.

Amir Zadeh, Paul Pu Liang, Navonil Mazumder, Soujanya Poria, Erik Cambria, and Louis-Philippe Morency. 2018. Memory fusion network for multiview sequential learning.

Appendix

A Evaluation Metrics

Consider $\{y_n\}_{n=1}^N$ as the true labels and $\{\hat{y}\}_{n=1}^N$ as the predicted labels for the N datapoints. Note that $y_n, \hat{y}_n \in \{1, 2, \ldots, K\}$ where K is the number of classes.

The **Accuracy score** for predictions if given by:

$$\text{Accuracy} = \frac{\sum_{n=1}^{N} \mathbb{I}\left[y_n = \hat{y}_n\right]}{N}$$

We use the `accuracy_score` method of Python based Scikit-learn library (Buitinck et al., 2013) for its evaluation. The **F1 score** for a class k is given by:

$$\text{F1}_k = \frac{2 \times \text{precision}_k \times \text{recall}_k}{\text{precision}_k + \text{recall}_k}$$

where, precision_k is the precision for class k and recall_k is the recall for class k. These are calculated using:

$$\text{precision}_k = \frac{\sum\limits_{\hat{y}_n = k} \mathbb{I}\left[y_n = \hat{y}_n\right]}{\sum\limits_{\hat{y}_n = k} 1}$$

$$\text{recall}_k = \frac{\sum\limits_{y_n = k} \mathbb{I}\left[y_n = \hat{y}_n\right]}{\sum\limits_{y_n = k} 1}$$

Finally, the **weighted F1 score** is defined as

$$\text{weighted F1} = \sum_{k=1}^{K} f_k \times \text{F1}_k$$

where f_k is the relative frequency of class k

We use the `F1_score` method of Scikit-learn library for its evaluation.

B Experiment Reproducibility

B.1 Input and hidden states dimensions

The Input modality dimensions for the different datasets we experimented are as follows:

CMU-MOSEI

- Text (BERT): 768
- Audio (OpenSmile): 384
- Video (OpenFace2.0): 711

IEMOCAP:

- Text (BERT): 768
- Audio (OpenSmile): 100
- Video (3D CNN): 512

The dimension of the hidden states and GRU states are as follows:

- Siamese hidden state ($\mathcal{H}_t$): 300
- Party state for each modality $s_t^{q_t,m}$: 150
- Context State for each modality c_t^m: 150
- Emotion State for each modality e_t^m: 100

All other weights and parameters are such that the equations given in §3 hold.

There are a total of 5578803 parameters in the model.

B.2 Training the main model

All experiments are implemented using the PyTorch library (Paszke et al., 2019). All weights are initialized randomly using PyTorch's default methods, and we use the Adam optimizer (Kingma and Ba, 2014) for training these weights.

The following hyper-parameters are used for the optimizer:

- Learning rate (lr) : 0.0001
- Weight decay (weight_decay): 0.0001
- β_1, β_2 (betas): (0.9, 0.999)

Here, the names in parenthesis denote the arguments corresponding to the hyper-parameters in the Adam Optimizer object of the PyTorch library.

We use a batch size of 128 for training across all experiments. The number of epochs for which the model was trained varies across datasets. These are listed as follows:

- CMU-MOSEI - 50 epochs
- IEMOCAP - 500 epochs

Training time per epoch was approximately 2.5 minutes for CMU-MOSEI and 15 seconds for IEMOCAP.

The model is evaluated at every epoch on the validation set (constructed using an 80:20 random split of the training data). The model giving the best weighted average F1 score across all classes is checkpointed. All the randomizations in the training procedure are reproducible using a seed value of 42 for libraries NumPy and PyTorch.

B.3 Training of the emotion shift component

This section provides the hyper-parameters for the pre-training procedure of the emotion shift component described in 4. We use a batch size of 8, and the model is pre-trained for five epochs. The model is checkpointed against the best F1 score.

B.4 Hyperparameter Tuning

Hyperparameters like the size of siamese hidden state ($\mathcal{H}_t$), size of context/party/hidden states ($s_t^{q_t,m}, c_t^m, e_t^m$) are tuned manually. The best weighted average F1 score over the validation set across all epochs was used as the criterion to select the best hyperparameter configuration.

To tune the hyperparameters used in the optimizer (learning rate, weight decay, β_1, β_2), we started with the default values used in the PyTorch library. These values are:

- learning rate: 0.001
- weight decay: 0
- β_1: 0.9
- β_2: 0.999

On manual tuning, we found that decreasing the learning rate to 0.0001 and increasing the weight decay to 0.0001 helped in better convergence and superior validation performance. Changing the values of β_1 and β_2 did not lead to any improvement. So these were kept the same as the default values.

B.5 Machine Specification

All experiments were performed on a server using Intel i7-5820K CPU @ 3.30GHz, Nvidia GeForce GTX TITAN X GPU, and CUDA 11.

Author Index

Association for Computational Linguistics
209 N. Eighth Street
Stroudsburg, Pennsylvania 18360

ISBN 978-1-7138-6192-8

CURRAN ASSOCIATES INC.
proceedings.com